Every modern-day, multitasking woma funny encouragement on a daily basis. with God will inspire you and urge you and reach out to God and others in new
—KERRI POMAROLLI, actress, comedian, and author
of *Guys Like Girls Named Jennie*

Swallowed. My. Gum. Pam Farrel and Dawn Wilson give some of those snort-laugh moments in *LOL with God*, all the while focusing us on Jesus with biblical practicality. *LOL with God* will help you grow in your faith and make you laugh hard. It's a fun, touching text-a-palooza!
—RHONDA RHEA, author of *Whatsoever Things Are Lovely*
and *High Heels in High Places*

With wit quicker than you can text LOL, these two BFFs, Pam and Dawn, take us to the only texting that really matters—God's Word. In a world of information overload, these gals encourage us to slow down and spend time with God as He speaks to our hearts about what's on His. This is a wonderful devotional for women on the go who long to sense God's presence throughout their busy days.
—SHARON JAYNES, author of *The Power of a Woman's Words*
and *Becoming Spiritually Beautiful*

Pam and Dawn will make you laugh, learn, and fall in love with God. Their high-tech humor will grab your attention and their heartfelt comments will bless your soul. Don't miss their incredible insights into life's most important issues.
—DR. ED HINDSON, Assistant Chancellor, Liberty University

Some people would lead you to believe that the only way to pursue a serious walk with God is to lose your sense of humor; but hilarity and worship have some strong common currents: a feeling of community, a loss of being so self-conscious, and a sense of surrender (have you ever tried to keep your arms crossed while laughing out loud? It isn't possible)! Apparently these people have never encountered such passages as, "Laughter does good like a medicine," or " . . . the joy of the Lord is your strength," or "God loves a cheerful giver." Pam Farrel and Dawn Wilson are true encouragers in every sense of the word. Throughout this book, as they encourage you to LOL while you are growing in your faith, open wide and prepare to receive your daily dose of laughter—that thing which "does good like a medicine."

—ANITA RENFROE, comedian and author of numerous projects, including *If It's Not One Thing, It's Your Mother* and *Don't Say I Didn't Warn You*

A cheerful heart is good medicine (Proverbs 17:22). Or as Mary Poppins said so eloquently, "A spoonful of sugar helps the medicine go down." Pam and Dawn have put together a spoonful of laughter to cheer your heart and to engage you in the word of God. You'll LOL and GTTTLFHIG! (Give Thanks To The Lord For He Is Good . . . I made that one up.)

—KENDRA SMILEY, author of *Journey of a Strong-Willed Child*

If God and Pam Farrel are both texting, it's time I joined them. And why not? The Great I AM is truly the Great IM. Pam's new daily devotional *LOL with God*, co-authored with Dawn Wilson, captures a contemporary pairing of earthly honesty and Living Words rolled into the deeper relationship we all seek with our Father in Heaven. This is gr8 stf!

—VIRELLE KIDDER, conference speaker and author of six books, including *Meet Me at the Well* and *The Best Life Ain't Easy*

Who knew it was possible to be both funny and profound at the same time? Laughing might be the best antioxidant to combat soul-toxins, don't you think? So, if a book can both tickle me and challenge me simultaneously, I want that book!

—JENNIFER KENNEDY DEAN, executive director of The Praying Life Foundation, author of numerous books, including the best-selling *Live a Praying Life*

Pam Farrel and Dawn Wilson have written a culturally relevant devotional that combines sound theology, relationship tips, and laugh-out-loud humor. For a daily dose of spiritual encouragement, read this book!

—CAROL KENT, speaker and author of *A New Kind of Normal*

LOL with GOD
devotional messages of hope & humor for women

Pam Farrel
Dawn Wilson

 Tyndale House Publishers, Inc.
Carol Stream, Illinois 60188

Pam Farrel is represented by the literary agency of Alive Communications Inc., 7680 Goddard Street, Suite 200, Colorado Springs, CO 80920, www.alivecommunications.com.

Library of Congress Cataloging-in-Publication Data
Farrel, Pam, 1959-
  LOL with God : messages of hope and humor for women / by Pam Farrel and Dawn Wilson.
    p. cm.
  ISBN 978-1-58997-345-9
  1. Christian women--Religious life. I. Wilson, Dawn. II. Title.
  BV4527.F476 2010
  248.8'43—dc22
                        2010010293

Printed in the United States of America
1 2 3 4 5 6 7 8 9 / 15 14 13 12 11 10

2 my gr8 hubby, Bill, 4 30 yrs of luv & LOL
(:-*, frm yr ^i^)
2 my bff, Dawn, 4 her wisdom & wrtng talent
(a, @>-->--, 4 u)
2 my 3 sons for yrs of LOL s2res
2 my bff joy zone team 4 hrd wrk wll done
2 the FOTF & Tyndale team 4 biLiVin wmn need 2 LOL w God.
2 my LOL wtg bffs & Seasoned Sisters who shared thr own LOL stories
2 my Lord 4 the Holy Text tht changed my life!
2 all r readRs, May God bring you gr8 joy!

—Pam

To Jesus—You fill my heart with purpose and joy. <3
To my loving husband, Bob—you are my dream-maker
and my best earthly friend. I love to LOL with you!
To my sons, Robert and Michael—I love you dearly,
and the families you lead so well. U ROK!
To every member of my supportive family, and every friend
who encouraged me to step beyond the borders of the ordinary—
HUGZ&THNX.
And to Pam Farrel, my co-author, mentor,
and friend—I am blessed to know you.
TY! UR AWSM GF!

—Dawn

Contents

Introduction

Hw do U kp a txtr in suspense? I'll tel U l8r.

If you understand the message above, you're probably a "texter." You love "texting"—writing text messages on your cell phone. If the words don't make sense to you yet, they will.

Part of understanding text messaging is to know some of the abbreviations. LOL is a familiar one. It stands for "laughing out loud." There are variations on that theme: FOTFLOL ("falling on the floor, laughing out loud") and ROTFL ("rolling on the floor, laughing").

We [Pam and Dawn] are avowed texters. We send text messages to our husbands, Bill and Bob, whenever we're on ministry trips in the United States and around the world. We appreciate the "instant" quality of text messaging; it's one way we keep in touch with those we love. The abbreviations and shortcuts of texting are fun, once a person learns the language.

Text-messaging with God—receiving His communications to us through His Word and sending our messages to Him in prayer—is more challenging. It involves more time, thought, and study.

What you'll find in this devotional are real-life stories with a splash of humor meant to brighten your day. The Bible tells us that "a cheerful heart is good medicine" (Proverbs 17:22), and the "joy of the Lord" is our strength (Nehemiah 8:10). It is our goal to try to tickle your funny bone in a way that will bring a smile to your face or maybe even make you giggle or laugh out loud. Even in secular reviews, humor is praised as a wonderful prescription. Years ago, *Saturday Review* editor Norman Cousins developed a debilitating disease, and doctors gave him only one chance in 500 of recovery. He increased his vitamin C, took aspirin liberally, and watched funny movies. "Hearty laughter," he said, "is a good way to jog internally without having to go outdoors."

In addition to real-life stories and humor, you'll discover some text messages from God's Word meant to strengthen and uplift your daily life. Jesus spoke words of hope so that His joy would overflow in His followers (John 17:13). The words of God remind people of His character and promises—and they are powerful to restore hope, vision, and joy. In Psalm 16:11 David says, "In Your presence is fullness of joy" (AMP), and it's our prayer that these texts will bring you joy, hope, and practical help to build your connection to the God who loves you.

To make it fun, we've added in text messages similar to those you might send and receive on your cell phone, but these will be from God's Word, so as you decode them, you'll feel empowered to handle whatever life sends your way.

So, ready to LOL? Then let's begin.

Virtual Disconnect

Text Message: *My hole bing follows hrd aftr U.* *

Our friend Gail is computer savvy. When she spends long work hours in front of the computer, Gail tells people, "I'm working on my monitor tan." That monitor tan isn't exclusive to computers.

Olivia Barker wrote about the "virtual glow" that texters and tweeters (Twitter writers) share as they gaze into the tiny windows of their Black-Berries.[1] Those addicted to cell phones, Facebook, Twitter, and other popular social-networking resources are buried so deeply in their virtual lives that they miss out on the real thing. Psychologist Kenneth Gergen calls it "absent presence." Texters and tweeters connect via a virtual connective thread, but they are physically absent. They network socially but often miss the warmth of a face-to-face relationship. Gergen worries that "the environment itself, that living world upon which our creatureliness is based, is separated from us."[2] In many cases, Barker writes, the wall of separation is a "glowing screen."

Christianity isn't a religion; it's a relationship. We are to "hold fast to the LORD" (Joshua 23:8) and "remain" in Christ's love (John 15:9). God desires face-to-face intimacy with us, but we're often sidetracked by pretty "glowing screens"—distractions that attract us and edge out the sense of God's presence. What gets in the way isn't always something bad. Even the urgency of Christian ministry can become a substitute for intimacy with God. We get so busy *doing* for God that we forget to simply *be* with Him.

Author and speaker Tom Elliff urges, "Don't lose sight of what it is to be with Jesus. . . . Each of us is as intimate with Christ as we choose to be."[3]

We're glad you're reading this devotional, but that's not even the same

---

* *My whole being follows hard after You and clings closely to You.* (Psalm 63:8, AMP)

as choosing intimacy with God. Even this book can become a "glowing screen" of distraction from sitting at Jesus' feet. We pray that you'll read and saturate your thoughts with God's words in the Bible (in the Text Helps section) and grow in your love for Him.

Stop right now, turn off all distractions—the computer, cell phone, TV, radio—and pause to pray and listen for the whisper of God.

❋ **Send Up a Message:** Father, help me sit humbly at Your feet—as close as I can get—listening to Your heart. Amen.

❋ **Text Helps:** Imagine what it must have been like for the disciples to walk and talk with Jesus, to learn from Him and seek His wisdom. Come to your quiet time alone with God in the same way. Think relationship, not duty. The following verses remind us how we can draw near to Him.

JOSHUA 23:8—But you are to hold fast to the LORD your God, as you have until now.

LUKE 10:38-39—As Jesus and his disciples were on their way, he came to a village where a woman named Martha opened her home to him. She had a sister called Mary, who sat at the Lord's feet listening to what he said.

HEBREWS 10:22—Let us draw near to God with a sincere heart in full assurance of faith.

❋ **Your Turn:** Write or text a message back to God about your life, what you read, or a request on your heart:

_____

_____

_____

_____

_____

_____

_____

LOL

In Working Order

It used to be that the biggest challenge connecting with someone long distance was finding a pay phone in working order. But now it appears to be human error. Sometimes *we* aren't in "working order."

For example, one friend of ours, Lynn, was having one of those days. She had a to-do list a mile long, and no way to get it all done in one day. While running from one errand to another, she decided to use her cell phone to call a girlfriend for some sympathy. The two friends commiserated over the bothersome consequences of constant multitasking.

As Lynn whined on the phone to her friend about her rough day, she arrived at her destination, gathered her purse, bags, and car keys, and shut the car door. Then she gasped to her friend, "Oh, no! Where's my cell phone?"

Her friend, caught up in Lynn's panic over losing something so vital, replied, "Did you look under the seat?"

Lynn reopened the car, searched, and said, "It's not there!"

The friend said, "How about checking your purse?"

Lynn dumped the contents out onto the parking lot, in a frenzied search for the missing item, but still no cell phone. Exasperated, Lynn shouted, "Lord, I've just got to find my cell! My son is going to call me any minute and tell me where to pick him up. Where is it?"

A pedestrian walking into the store overheard Lynn's frantic plea and said calmly, "You're talking on it."[4]

1. Olivia Barker, "Got That Virtual Glow?" Life, *USA Today*, sec. D, www.usatoday.com/printedition/life/20090803/livingmoment03_cv.art.htm (accessed March 10, 2010).
2. Ibid.
3. Tom Elliff, "Intimacy with Christ," Life Action Revival Ministries (podcast, October 21, 2009), www.lifeaction.org/infuse-podcast/2009/10/21/intimacy-christ/ (accessed March 10, 2010).
4. Personal story shared with authors. Used by permission.

IM Illiterate

Text Message: *Schl me n yr wys.* *

Abbreviations came easy in grade school, but I [Dawn] sure have struggled with IM (instant messaging) abbreviations. Used in chatting and text messaging, they're like a foreign language, and I confess, IM illiterate.

My friend Gail used OTOH in a recent chat.

"Say what?" I broke in.

She explained, "Oh, you didn't know that? It means 'on the other hand.'"

The problem is, with people like me who have a limited IM vocabulary, it takes more time to *explain* the abbreviation than to simply type in the phrase it represents. So I'm memorizing an IM abbreviation list. I don't know *when* I'll use ADIP (another day in paradise) or HTNOTH (hit the nail on the head), but I'm ready!

When my husband is traveling in foreign countries, we use simple texting abbreviations to save time—phrases you might see on a vanity car license, like "b4" and "gr8." We sprinkle our messages with LOL (laughing out loud), BTW (by the way), and TTYL (talk to you later). Anything longer would require explanations; he's IM illiterate too.

It's not just abbreviations that trip me up; it's trying to speed up my texting. I'm amazed by the tweens-to-20s who seem to text at the speed of light. Seventeen-year-old Elliot Nicholls typed the text message "The razor-toothed piranhas of the genera serrasalmus and pygocentrus are the most ferocious freshwater fish in the world. In reality, they seldom attack a human" in only 45 seconds, without looking at his screen and without any mistakes! Another teen, Morgan Pozgar, typed the Mary Poppins word *supercalifragilisticexpialidocious* in 15 seconds

---

* *Show me how you work, God; school me in your ways.* (Psalm 25:4, MSG)

flat![1] Thumb athletes from 13 countries competed in texting in January 2010, and the winners—two teens from South Korea—took home a $100,000 prize.[2] Whew! Whether it's abbreviations or speed-texting, I've got a lot to learn!

I'm glad that God didn't abbreviate anything. In His Word He carefully and clearly spelled out who He is and what He expects. He knew that with all of the false teachers in our world, we'd need plain answers that square with His character and standards. And He's more concerned with us understanding the Truth than speeding through His Word.

My husband says, "God doesn't hide His will like Easter eggs." God makes most of our choices plain—good or evil, truth or error. If we trust and honor Him and seek His wisdom, He will show us how to live right. He'll not only give us light for our everyday decisions (Psalm 119:130), but He'll also teach us how to use His Word to answer questions others ask and create a hunger for Him.

Yes, the more we know God's Word, the more we'll speak His language.

✳ **Send Up a Message:** Father God, Your Word is clear. Teach me Your ways, and I will obey. Amen.

✳ **Text Helps:** We have the ability to understand the Bible because it is God-breathed, and the Spirit of God dwells within the believer to shed light on God's Word. Take a look at the following verses. Remember that learning from Scripture is an ongoing process. God *wants* you to know Him.

PSALM 25:4-5—Show me your ways, O LORD, teach me your paths; guide me in your truth and teach me, for you are God my Savior, and my hope is in you all day long.

PSALM 119:33-35—Teach me, O LORD, to follow your decrees; then I will keep them to the end. Give me understanding, and I will keep your law and obey it with all my heart. Direct me in the path of your commands, for there I find delight.

PSALM 119:130—The unfolding of your words gives light; it gives understanding to the simple.

PROVERBS 3:5-6—Trust in the LORD with all your heart and lean not on your own understanding; in all your ways acknowledge him, and he will make your paths straight.

❋ **Your Turn:** Write or text a message back to God about your life, what you read, or a request on your heart:

_____

_____

_____

_____

_____

_____

LOL

Textiquette

1. Learn when and where it's appropriate to text. Here's a hint: If you're in a place where texting would be considered rude or inappropriate, don't text. If you're in a situation where those around you will feel ignored or less valued if you text, don't text. If anyone's life, including your own, will be endangered by your texting (such as driving while texting!), don't text. If someone is paying you for your time, don't use that time to carry on a private texting conversation.
2. Prioritize being with people over texting. A real live conversation should trump a texting one any day.
3. The more important the topic of conversation, the more likely you should talk to the person live or by phone. Also, the more emotional the content, the less techie the method of communication should be. For example, don't break off a relationship via a text message! (The husband of one of my [Pam's] friends texted her that he was leaving her for another woman!)
4. Don't set an annoying alarm to go off every time a text arrives, or your friends and family might just take your phone and throw it against the wall.

5. Don't send any messages, abbreviations, photos, or graphics that would embarrass you if your mother looked over your shoulder. Better yet, remember that God sees and knows all things!

6. Keep text messages short and simple. Here are a few common texting shortcuts:

BFF—"best friends forever"	J/K—"just kidding"
BTW—"by the way"	KWIM—"know what I mean?"
BHL8—"be home late"	OTL—"out to lunch"
FTF or F2F—"face-to-face"	RME—"rolling my eyes"
F2T?—"free to talk?"	RUOK—"are you okay?"
GF—"girlfriend"	TTFN—"ta ta for now"
GMTA—"great minds think alike"	W84M—"wait for me"

1. "New Fastest Texting Record Set by Teen," Geeksugar, November 21, 2007, www.geeksugar.com/New-Fastest-Texting-Record-Set-Teen-827128 (accessed March 10, 2010).

2. Verena Dobnik, "How Fast Can U Text? Thumb Athletes from 13 Countries Compete in NY," Associated Press, MSN Tech and Gadgets, January 14, 2010, http://tech.ca.msn.com/canadianpress-article.aspx?cp-documentid=23259002 (accessed March 10, 2010).

God's Text Message

Text Message: *R God's Wd stds frm & 4evr.* *

Americans love to communicate, whether by text messaging, instant messaging (IM), or Skype. CTIA (Cellular Telecommunications Industry Association) CEO Steve Largent said U.S. wireless subscribers sent a staggering one trillion SMS (short message service) messages in 2008, triple the quantity sent in 2007—363 billion.[1] Gartner, an information technology research firm, predicts the number of text messages will increase to 2.3 trillion in 2010.[2]

God also loves to communicate. He spoke directly to the Patriarchs, spoke in dreams and visions to the ancient prophets, spoke through the Holy Spirit to "holy men of God" (2 Peter 1:21, KJV), and ultimately, spoke through the living Word, His Son (Hebrews 1:1, KJV). The written Word is God's grand text message to the world, a record of who He is. Over and over we hear the phrase "Thus saith the LORD" in Scripture.

God can use a pastor, a friend, a book, or some other means to speak to our hearts and motivate us to live for Him, but none of their messages can be contrary to God's Word. I [Dawn] love self-help books because I've learned so much about leadership, relationships, communication, and personal growth from them. A person can find a book on just about any self-help topic imaginable. Many self-help books focus on taking control of our lives, fixing our problems, and improving ourselves so we'll be more successful, more accepted, and so on. Self-help books written from a Christian perspective remind us that only God can fix, heal, and help us. Unfortunately, for a long time I focused on self-help books and neglected the Word of God. I finally realized I needed more of *God's* help, not self-help.

---

*Our God's Word stands firm and forever. (Isaiah 40:8, MSG)

Remember, God's Word is our authority and guide. It's relevant for every generation. It's powerful and true. It's also the voice of hope, comfort, and peace, and the source of strength for everyday problems.

God's message will never be erased. His Word is eternal; it lives and abides forever.

❋ **Send Up a Message:** Thank You, Father, for the Bible—holy, loving, and powerful. It speaks to my heart. Amen.

❋ **Text Helps:** The Word of God can change your life. It's not an ordinary book. Thank God for the precious gift of His Word as you read the following verses.

   1 CORINTHIANS 10:11—These things happened to them [God's people] as examples and were written down as warnings for us, on whom the fulfillment of the ages has come.

   1 THESSALONIANS 2:13—We also thank God continually because, when you received the word of God, which you heard from us, you accepted it not as the word of men, but as it actually is, the word of God, which is at work in you who believe.

   2 PETER 1:21—Prophecy never had its origin in the will of man, but men spoke from God as they were carried along by the Holy Spirit.

❋ **Your Turn:** Write or text a message back to God about your life, what you read, or a request on your heart:

_____

_____

_____

_____

_____

_____

_____

_____

_____

LOL

Saying Prayers

Pat Brumble's six-year-old granddaughter Brandy loved to spend the night at her "Mimi's" house. At night before falling asleep, Pat would listen to Brandy say her prayers. As she prayed, Brandy mentioned practically everyone she'd ever met, but Pat didn't mind the lengthy recitation.

One night after Brandy finally said, "Amen," Pat said, "That was a beautiful prayer!"

Brandy sat up straight in the bed and said, "I've got another one. Wanna hear it?"[3]

1. Newlaunches.com, "Americans sent 1 trillion text messages in 2008," posted 4-3-09 by dhiram, http://www.newlaunches.com/archives/americans_sent_1_trillion_text_messages_in_2008.php (accessed March 23, 2010).

2. Estimate cited in "2.3 Trillion Text Messages Sent by 2010," posted by ZDNet Research on IT Facts, Alex Moskalyuk, December 12, 2006, http://blogs.zdnet.com/ITFacts/?p=12176 (accessed March 10, 2010).

3. Pat Brumble's personal story. Used by permission.

Influence

Text Message: *B mrcifl jst s ur Fthr s mrcifl.***

According to www.friendshipstats.com, I [Pam], after four months on Facebook, have 329 friends. If I contracted a deadly variant of flu, I would likely infect 11 people. If I died today, an estimated 464 people would try to attend my funeral. Based on my Facebook profile, I have a 91 percent probability of getting married—which is good, since I've been happily married 30 years. Though this is just the Facebook influence, it serves as an example that we *all* have influence.

In *Woman of Influence* I describe influence in this way:

> Measuring the full impact of influence is nearly impossible. When I was a little girl, I loved to pick the dandelions when they were fluffy and white. I'd blow, and hundreds of little helicopters would fly into the air. I tried to watch where they all went, but as they got caught in the breeze, many would blow higher and higher until they disappeared. Just like those seeds, influence often isn't noticed until it blossoms later in the garden of someone else's life.[1]

What are you doing to extend your influence? Do you speak a word of encouragement to those you meet along the pathways of your world—perhaps a teacher, coach, doctor, dry cleaner attendant, doorman, waiter, or manicurist? Imagine how your words might motivate someone to try harder or make better choices. Can you remember a time in your own life when someone in a position of influence encouraged you? How did it change your attitudes or actions?

---

* *Be merciful, just as your Father is merciful.* (Luke 6:36)

Look at the fringes of your life and touch someone new with kindness. Influence is simple to extend; just care for someone new today.

✳ **Send Up a Message:** Lord, help me see and care for those You place in my path today. Amen.

✳ **Text Helps:** Kindness shows up in different ways. Sometimes it looks like serving; sometimes it looks like giving; sometimes it looks like encouragement or love. As you read the following verses, look for some ways you can express kindness.

> LUKE 6:30-38—Give to everyone who asks you, and if anyone takes what belongs to you, do not demand it back. Do to others as you would have them do to you. If you love those who love you, what credit is that to you? Even "sinners" love those who love them. And if you do good to those who are good to you, what credit is that to you? Even "sinners" do that. And if you lend to those from whom you expect repayment, what credit is that to you? Even "sinners" lend to "sinners," expecting to be repaid in full. But love your enemies, do good to them, and lend to them without expecting to get anything back. Then your reward will be great, and you will be sons of the Most High, because he is kind to the ungrateful and wicked. Be merciful, just as your Father is merciful. Do not judge, and you will not be judged. Do not condemn, and you will not be condemned. Forgive, and you will be forgiven. Give, and it will be given to you. A good measure, pressed down, shaken together and running over, will be poured into your lap. For with the measure you use, it will be measured to you.

✳ **Your Turn:** Write or text a message back to God about your life, what you read, or a request on your heart:

_____

_____

_____

_____

LOL

Promoted

Like many authors, Sandra Aldrich has a heart for military families, who have their own unique challenges. She told us this delightful story about one such family:

> One of our military friends, Joe, couldn't wait to tell his family he had been promoted from captain to major. When he walked through the back door of his home, his seven-year-old daughter, Betsy, was at the kitchen table coloring. As she looked up to greet him, he said, "Betsy, guess what I became today?"
>
> She took one look at his happy expression and squealed, "You're president of the United States!"
>
> How do you confess you're only a major after that?[2]

---

1. Pam Farrel, *Woman of Influence: Ten Traits of Those Who Want to Make a Difference* (Downers Grove, IL: InterVarsity Press, 1996), 8.
2. Sandra Aldrich, personal story shared with authors. Used by permission.

Joy Hunt

Text Message: *Ask & u wl rcve & ur joy w b cmplt.* *

When days are bleak, the pressure is on, or disappointments are on a roll, Bill and I [Pam] have a habit of trading jokes, e-mailing humor, or sliding funny cards into each other's luggage or under our office doors. We also go on a joy hunt. We look for and share humor along our daily path, such as Bill forgetting a pair of suit pants when performing a wedding—almost the only thing a pastor needs to make sure he has in his possession when officiating nuptials.

The Bible is packed with verses that can help us unearth joy. We can use these tools to discover and hold on to our joy. Consider the practical truths in these power-packed verses:

- 1 Chronicles 16:27—"Strength and joy [are] in his dwelling place." *(Dwell with God and find joy!)*
- Job 33:26—"He prays to God and finds favor with him, he sees God's face and shouts for joy." *(Pray, and joy will be reignited.)*
- Psalm 5:11—"Let all who take refuge in you be glad; let them ever sing for joy." *(Hide your heart in God, and joy will erupt in song.)*
- Psalm 35:27—"May those who delight in my vindication shout for joy and gladness; may they always say, 'The LORD be exalted, who delights in the well-being of his servant.'" *(Rejoice in God's righteousness, and justice and joy will return.)*
- Psalm 71:23—"My lips will shout for joy when I sing praise to you—I, whom you have redeemed." *(Worship God for His redeeming love, and joy will naturally evolve.)*

---

* *"Ask and you will receive, and your joy will be complete."* (John 16:24)

- Psalm 92:4—"You make me glad by your deeds, O LORD; I sing for joy at the works of your hands." *(Review the goodness of God, and joy will fill your mind and roll off your lips.)*
- Psalm 118:15—"Shouts of joy and victory resound in the tents of the righteous: 'The LORD's right hand has done mighty things!'" *(Review God's victories, and joy will accompany the rerun of love.)*
- Psalm 145:7—"They will celebrate your abundant goodness and joyfully sing of your righteousness." *(Throw a party to celebrate God's provision, and joy will be the centerpiece of your life.)*
- Proverbs 21:15—"When justice is done, it brings joy to the righteous." *(Do the right thing, and joy will stick.)*
- Jeremiah 15:16—"When your words came, I ate them; they were my joy and my heart's delight." *(Get into God's Word—joy is there!)*

Joy is a journey. Take a step toward Jesus to begin your vacation of the heart.

✸ **Send Up a Message:** Lord, give me Your joy today, even in difficult situations. Amen.

✸ **Text Helps:** The first verse in the following Scripture quotes reminds us that true joy is found in God's presence. We experience joy as we · abide in Him. The second scripture commands us to be joyful as we worship the Lord. The last verse tells us how to have complete joy.

PSALM 16:11—You have made known to me the path of life; you will fill me with joy in your presence, with eternal pleasures at your right hand.

PSALM 100—Shout for joy to the LORD, all the earth. Worship the LORD with gladness; come before him with joyful songs. Know that the LORD is God. It is he who made us, and we are his; we are his people, the sheep of his pasture. Enter his gates with thanksgiving and his courts with praise; give thanks to him and praise his name. For the LORD is good and his love endures forever; his faithfulness continues through all generations.

JOHN 15:10-11—[Jesus said,] "If you obey my commands, you will remain in my love, just as I have obeyed my Father's commands and remain in his love. I have told you this so that my joy may be in you and that your joy may be complete."

❋ **Your Turn:** Write or text a message back to God about your life, what you read, or a request on your heart:

_____

_____

_____

_____

_____

_____

LOL

Laughing in the Moment!

Sometimes finding extra space in our homes is easier than adjusting to the change that can come with it . . .

When I [Dawn] brought our second son, Michael, home from the hospital, I expected that my husband and I would have to make some adjustments. We made room for "Mikey" in our hearts and in our small apartment, and he grew up to be a relatively quiet little boy. But that wasn't the case early on.

It didn't take long to realize our first son, Robert, had some adjustments to make too. The first time Michael let loose with a long, loud wail, Robert's eyes widened and he clapped his hands over his ears.

"Oh, no," he yelled. "Do we have to *keep* him?"

Eating the Word

Text Message: *I rjoic @ Yr wd.* *

My [Dawn's] favorite Bible is not only dog-eared; it's dog-chewed. Back in my college days, my old cockapoo, Muffin, decided the red leather cover was tastier than his chew toy, and my poor Bible was never the same. Next to one corner of the damaged cover, on the inside flap, I later wrote, "Thy words were found, and I did eat them" (Jeremiah 15:16, KJV).

I wore the Bible out at Bible college and in a revival ministry. The binding is broken, and frayed pages stick out unevenly. Inside, the front and back pages are crammed with quotations and references, and my underlining has bled through the delicate onion-skin paper. Whole pages are Scotch-taped in place. Yet even though it's fragile and worn, it's still my favorite Bible.

Several Christmases ago, my youngest son and his wife bought me an exact replacement, but with thicker pages. I'm slowly transferring my notes. Someday I'll give my older son my original Bible, and return the newer Bible with the copied notes to my younger son. As far as I'm concerned, these will be my most valuable gifts to them.

I [Pam] also mark significant passages in the margins of my Bible, such as "Helped me decide to marry Bill"; "Gave answer to struggle in raising Zach and his ADD"; "Gave hope in depression." I also like to color-code passages, highlighting verbs, commands, or promises in various shades.

The Word of God lasts forever, and we pray that it will guide and nourish the lives of those we love as it has our lives. The blessing of my [Dawn's] "eaten" Bible is that God has used the study of His Word in my life not only for personal edification but for ministry to others. The

---

* *I rejoice at Your word as one who finds great treasure.* (Psalm 119:162, NKJV)

blessing of my [Pam's] color-coded Bible is that it has benefited not just me but all those who have heard my teaching or read any of my books.

Some years after Muffin used my Bible as a chew toy, I [Dawn] added the second part of Jeremiah 15:16 near the dog-eaten corner: "And Your word was to me the joy and rejoicing of my heart" (NKJV).

Are you "eating" the Word, letting it nourish you and bless your heart?

✳ **Send Up a Message:** Your Word is a treasure, Lord. It fills and satisfies my soul. Amen.

✳ **Text Helps:** Think of how many times a day you nourish your physical body. Now, how often do you "eat" the Word of God? You need spiritual nourishment, too! As you read the following scriptures, ask God to make you hungry for His Word.

PSALM 34:8—Taste and see that the LORD is good.

PSALM 145:16—You open your hand and satisfy the desires of every living thing.

MATTHEW 4:4—Jesus answered, "It is written: 'Man does not live on bread alone, but on every word that comes from the mouth of God.'"

MATTHEW 5:6—Blessed are those who hunger and thirst for righteousness, for they will be filled.

✳ **Your Turn:** Write or text a message back to God about your life, what you read, or a request on your heart:

_____

_____

_____

_____

_____

_____

_____

LOL

Hungry for God

When Bill and I [Pam] were young parents, we hung on the door of each of our children's rooms their "name verse," which explained what their names meant and displayed a Bible verse that reflected the definition. We did this so our sons would know what we prayed they would become.

As young parents, we were also youth pastors, and as a tired mom of toddlers, I enjoyed church "afterglows" because our sons were well looked after by a host of loving people. I tried to keep an eye on my boys, but I didn't always know exactly who had which son at any given moment.

One night during a celebration in the church gym, an excited teen came running over to me and said, "Do you know where Zach is?"

I looked around, and not spotting him, I said in a panic, "No. Do you?"

"Yes, he's over there eating someone's Bible!"

I ran across the gym to find my baby sitting on the floor, gulping down a page out of a Bible. I quickly realized it belonged to Pastor Doug.

I took the chewed-up piece of paper out of the mouth of my hungry son and tucked it into my pants pocket, picked up the baby and the Bible, and sprinted across the gym to Pastor Doug.

"Doug, I am so sorry! Zach . . . um, well, he's eaten part of your Bible."

Doug, with a broad smile, replied, "I bet he ate 1 Corinthians 13, and I'll just have to love him!"

I pulled the tattered, wet portion of Scripture out of my pocket to reveal that indeed it was 1 Corinthians 13—or at least part of it—that Zach had consumed.

Oh, and Zach's name verse is:

Zach: the LORD has remembered

"You understand, O LORD;

remember me and care for me. . . .

When your words came, I ate them;

they were my joy and my heart's delight."

(Jeremiah 15:15, 16)

What's a Single Girl to Do?

Text Message: *Kp urslves in Gods luv as u w8.* *

Single women often ask us what they should do while they wait for Mr. Right to come along. The Christian life is all about waiting. Verse 21 of Jude encourages believers to "keep yourselves in God's love as you wait for the mercy of our Lord Jesus Christ to bring you to eternal life." Marriage doesn't "complete" our lives; God does. God has plenty for us women to do, whether we're single or married:

- *Be a light.* Seek to bring glory to God (Matthew 5:16; 1 Corinthians 6:20; 1 Peter 4:16).
- *Be a servant.* Help people and put others' needs above your own desires (Matthew 22:39; Mark 9:35; Philippians 2:3-4).
- *Be pure.* Seek to live a life of sexual purity (Exodus 20:14; Acts 15:20; 1 Corinthians 6:18; 1 Corinthians 7:2).
- *Be an example.* Live so that others can step in your footprints and find God. Let your lifestyle be one that reflects moral strength (1 Timothy 4:12; Titus 2:7-8; 1 Peter 2:12).
- *Be a woman of the Word.* Base your life on God's Word, know what you believe, and be able to defend those beliefs from Scripture (Acts 17:11; 2 Timothy 2:15; 1 Peter 3:15).
- *Be content.* Find happiness in the circumstances in which God has placed you. Nothing is more attractive than a happy, content woman (Psalm 73:25; 1 Corinthians 7:7-8, 27, 34; Philippians 4:11; 1 Thessalonians 5:18; 1 Timothy 6:6-8).

---

* *Keep yourselves in God's love as you wait.* (Jude, verse 21)

- *Be active.* Use your gifts, skills, and talents to live out the adventure God has designed for you. It's often on the path of pursuing God that you'll meet Mr. Right. One thing's for sure: fulfillment is found on the journey of living out your uniqueness (Romans 12:5-8; 1 Corinthians 12; 1 Corinthians 14:1). If you need help discovering your uniqueness or gaining courage to step out in your adventure, I [Pam] offer more insights in *Woman of Confidence: Step into God's Adventure for Your Life* and *The 10 Best Decisions a Woman Can Make.*

The best decision any woman can make is to discover who God made her to be and then live it out. Be a quality woman, and quality people of both genders will want to spend time with wonderful, quality you!

✽ **Send Up a Message:** Lord, help me be and do now what You have designed for me. Don't let me sit around waiting for life to begin when it already has. Amen.

✽ **Text Helps:** What are you waiting for? God has an incredible adventure planned for your life! Allow these verses to speak to your heart.

MATTHEW 5:16—Let your light shine before men, that they may see your good deeds and praise your Father in heaven.

1 TIMOTHY 4:12—Don't let anyone look down on you because you are young, but set an example for the believers in speech, in life, in love, in faith and in purity.

2 TIMOTHY 2:15—Do your best to present yourself to God as one approved, a workman who does not need to be ashamed and who correctly handles the word of truth.

PHILIPPIANS 4:11—I have learned to be content whatever the circumstances.

✽ **Your Turn:** Write or text a message back to God about your life, what you read, or a request on your heart:

_____

_____

_____

_____

LOL

Ways to Know God's Will for Your Life

Consecrate your will to God—Surrender to God, seeking and *doing* (obeying) His will first!

Commit to the Word of God—Meditate on Scripture. God's Word won't contradict His will.

Commune with God in prayer—Rest in His presence, listening for His voice.

Contemplate godly counsel—Follow counselors' biblical advice, not just opinions.

Check out circumstances—Examine open and closed "doors" as *possible* direction.

Connect to God's desires—Ask God to align your heart with His perspective and plans.

Consider common sense—God gave you a brain; you need to use it. Think things through before making decisions.

Confidently move forward with courage—Set wise goals and pursue them with confidence.

The Bigger the Battle, the Bigger the Blessing

Text Message: *Blsed s th 1 who prsvers . . . u wl recv th crown.**

I [Pam] had one baby and a toddler and was four months pregnant, dressed in a white suit as I carefully stepped out of my house to head to Bible study. A heavy rainstorm had hit the night before, and there was a film of red clay mud all down the front stairs.

With a toddler, diaper bag, and Bible-study bag in tow, I gingerly stepped onto the first stair, holding on to the handrail. Then, I gingerly took step two, only to fall flat on my back, desperately clinging to my baby to keep him from hitting his head. Sliding down the rest of the stairs, I finally plopped in a puddle on the bottom landing.

Shaken, I stood up and checked on baby Brock, who was smiling from the adventurous ride and seemed completely unharmed. Once relief set in that he had survived the fall, I burst into tears. Fear gripped my heart. *Lord, what about this baby inside me? A fall like this can cause a miscarriage. Please protect this little one!*

I took inventory of my belongings, spilled across the lawn and the stairs. I would have to take a wet rag to most of the things, but they all seemed intact. Then I looked at myself in the reflection of our bay window. I was one big mud pie, head to toe. I checked my watch. If I took the time to clean up, I would definitely be late to Bible study. Then a thought came: *Maybe I should just stay home.*

Remembering Ephesians 6:11-13 about life being a spiritual battle, I

---

* *Blessed is the man who perseveres under trial, because when he has stood the test, he will receive the crown of life that God has promised to those who love him.* (James 1:12)

loudly proclaimed, "Satan, get out of here! If you think a little mud or a tumble is going to keep me from God's Word, you are messing with the wrong woman. I take my stand in Jesus and through His shed blood, I claim the victory. If you're working this hard to discourage me, Satan, then something really great is on the other side, if I persevere. The bigger the battle, the bigger the blessing on the other side!"

With that, I got up, went inside to change clothes, and then drove to Bible study, where I *did* receive more encouragement to win the battles of life.

I'm glad I learned that lesson long ago, because during the writing of this devotional, I think nearly everything I own broke: my car, my computer (it crashed twice), the ice-maker, the washing machine, the printers in our office—and more importantly, the hearts of two of my three sons. This mom was carrying their pain on her heart.

During this same time, Dawn had equal trials of illness, family members in pain, and equipment malfunctions and breakdowns. But we both know we'll receive a blessing if we press on through the battle.

Press on! Blessings ahead!

❋ **Send Up a Message:** Lord, help me not to give in to the battle weariness I feel. Keep my eyes off the attack and on You, the One who gives victory and blessing. Amen.

❋ **Text Helps:** We can stand strong and move forward valiantly because Jesus has already overcome our enemy (read Matthew 4:1-11). The following verses encourage you to press on in the battle.

EPHESIANS 6:11-13—Put on the full armor of God so that you can take your stand against the devil's schemes. For our struggle is not against flesh and blood, but against the rulers, against the authorities, against the powers of this dark world and against the spiritual forces of evil in the heavenly realms. Therefore put on the full armor of God, so that when the day of evil comes, you may be able to stand your ground, and after you have done everything, to stand.

PHILIPPIANS 3:12-14—Not that I have already obtained all this, or have already been made perfect, but I press on to take hold of that for which Christ Jesus took hold of me. Brothers, I do not consider myself yet to have taken hold of it. But one thing I do: Forgetting what is behind and straining toward what is ahead, I press on toward the goal to win the prize for which God has called me heavenward in Christ Jesus.

2 TIMOTHY 2:3—Endure hardship with us like a good soldier of Christ Jesus.

❋ **Your Turn:** Write or text a message back to God about your life, what you read, or a request on your heart:

_____

_____

_____

_____

LOL

Super Baby

One day, when Zach was about 18 months old, I [Pam] laid him down for a nap. I thought he was asleep, but I soon heard noises coming from his room. I walked to his nursery and peered through the doorway at a scene that looked like something from Bing Crosby's *White Christmas*. Zach had somehow climbed out of his crib and then swung over onto his changing table using a three-tiered basket as the "rope." As I entered the room, he was shaking two full bottles of baby powder all over his room, all over his bed, and all over himself.

I dusted Zach off, took him to my room, and sat him on my bed. With my sternest voice and the meanest face I could muster, I said, "Zachery Jonathan Farrel, I want you to stay right here on this bed. Is that clear, Zachery?"

I turned to go back to the nursery and somehow clean up the blizzard. I mopped up as much of the white powder as I could and then returned to my room. Zach wasn't on the bed. Then I heard giggles—and I peeked into my bathroom. Zach had gotten under the sink and taken out an entire box of tampons. He'd stuffed them like firecrackers out of the top of his diaper. He'd also taken my sanitary pads and stuck them all over his little body. He was so proud of himself. He was beaming from ear to ear when I entered.

Throwing his hands up over his head, he yelled, "Look, Mom, stickers!"

Say "Yes!"

Text Message: *"Do u bleve tht I m abl 2 do ths?"*
*Thy sd 2 Him, "Ys, Lord."**

This is the year of my [Pam's] "jubilee"—the 50th year of my life—so I've reflected on the most important decisions I've made over the years that lifted my life out of the "pit" of family pain and dysfunction I was born into. As I've reflected on the positive moments of forward movement, every decision can be traced back to what I call "listening to the whisper of God."

John 14:26 explains, "The Counselor, the Holy Spirit, whom the Father will send in my name, will teach you all things and will remind you of everything I have said to you." And "When he, the Spirit of truth, comes, he will guide you into all truth" (John 16:13). The whisper isn't an audible voice but an inner push toward obeying God's Word.

I was 8 when I first heard the Spirit whisper to my heart that God loved me and wanted a relationship with me. That relationship with God would be my way to wholeness and help in creating a new life.

I was 18 when I heard the Spirit whisper to me that I needed to make better choices in whom and how I dated, so I decided not to date anyone who didn't share my faith in Jesus. That same year while I was in college, my friend Grace invited me to join a Bible study on campus. I heard the Spirit whisper, "Go for it!" It was there I met a mentor who was willing to invest her time to help me remake my life from the inside out.

That year, the Spirit whispered to me one challenge after another:

"Pam, *read* God's Word daily—and Pam, *do* what it says, no matter if you feel afraid. I will help you with that fear, if you step out and obey."

---

* *[Jesus said to His disciples,] "Do you believe that I am able to do this?" They said to Him, "Yes, Lord."* (Matthew 9:28, NASB)

"Pam, *go* to that leadership conference—and Pam, see that guy across the lobby? *Talk to him.*"

"Pam, *share* your new faith every day with someone."

"Pam, you know that guy you met at the leadership conference? *Say 'Yes!'* when he asks you on a date—and *date with integrity and purity.*"

"Pam, spend the summer at a Bible institute."

"Pam, I am calling you into ministry."

"*Say 'Yes!'* Pam, when Bill proposes."

"Pam, I am calling you and Bill into youth ministry. *Say 'Yes!'*"

"Pam, I am calling you and Bill to Bible college and seminary. It will be a big move to a scary city, but *say 'Yes!'*"

"Pam, I am calling you and Bill to teach on relationships. *Say 'Yes!'*"

"Pam, I am calling you and Bill to be parents. *Say 'Yes!'* Before the baby is born, I want both of you to *read* my Word and all kinds of parenting books to relearn what a healthy family is. *Say 'Yes!'*"

And every time I said "Yes!" to God's Spirit, life took a turn upward.

✻ **Send Up a Message:** Lord, help me say "Yes!" to Your whisper. Amen.

✻ **Text Helps:** Knowing about, listening to, and obeying God's Spirit is so powerful in helping to move your life and relationships forward. The following verses will help you discover more about who the Holy Spirit is and what He can do for you.

JOHN 14:16-17—*(The Spirit stays with You.)* [Jesus said,] "I will ask the Father, and He will give you another Helper, that He may be with you forever; that is the Spirit of truth, whom the world cannot receive, because it does not see Him or know Him, but you know Him because He abides with you and will be in you." (NASB)

JOHN 15:26—*(The Spirit teaches you about God.)* [Jesus said,] "When the Helper comes, whom I will send to you from the Father, that is the Spirit of truth who proceeds from the Father, He will testify about Me." (NASB)

JOHN 16:13—*(The Spirit leads you in truth.)* When He, the Spirit of truth, comes, He will guide you into all the truth. (NASB)

ROMANS 8:26—*(The Spirit translates your prayers.)* The Spirit also helps our weakness; for we do not know how to pray as we should, but the Spirit Himself intercedes for us with groanings too deep for words. (NASB)

1 CORINTHIANS 2:10—*(The Spirit reveals the things of God to you.)* To us God revealed them through the Spirit; for the Spirit searches all things, even the depths of God. (NASB)

❋ **Your Turn:** Write or text a message back to God about your life, what you read, or a request on your heart:

_____

_____

_____

_____

_____

LOL

A Closer Look

After my [Dawn's] brother- and sister-in-law, Tom and Janice, enjoyed dinner with friends at a restaurant in San Diego, the waitress brought the bill. She mentioned how glad she was that Tom and Janice and their friends had prayed before they ate their meal. That simple act of prayer had been an encouragement and testimony to her.

Then she shared a story:

A few days earlier, she was waiting on a table of 10 people. After a short time, the manager asked her why she hadn't taken their order yet.

"They all have their hands close to their chests, and their heads are bowed," she said. "They're praying, and I don't want to disturb them."

"No," the manager said. "Look closer."

The waitress then realized that they weren't praying; they were all on their cell phones, texting people.

❋ ❋ ❋

Times Like These

Text Message: *Who nos whthr u hv cm 2 t kngdm 4 sch a tm s ths?**

Hundreds died in 1977 when two jumbo jets collided on the runway of Los Rodeos airport in Tenerife in the Canary Islands.[1] Weeping as I [Dawn] watched the news, I remember saying, "I don't think I want to bring a child into such a dangerous, scary world." Considering that I was pregnant at the time, I didn't have much choice in the matter.

Unfortunately, the world is an even scarier place today with terrorists and economic upheaval. But the truth is, there has never been a safe time on earth, and we'll never find complete security here apart from the Lord.

God often gives courage to His people to accomplish His purposes. He used Jacob's son Joseph in scary times to help His people flourish during a severe famine in Egypt (Genesis 41; 50:20).

Jochebed feared for her infant son's life when she heard Pharaoh's cruel edict that all male babies must die, but this resourceful, faith-filled mom saved her boy, and Moses rose to lead a nation (Exodus 1:15–2:10; 6:1-7, 20).

And don't forget the story of courageous Queen Esther, who understood the perils of standing against the enemy of the Jews but heeded her cousin's wise suggestion that God may have called her to save His people from harm (Esther 4:14).

When I [Pam] am afraid, I review Scripture verses that reveal God's power, protection, and provision. His Word is the light for my fearful soul. Like those times as a little girl when I was afraid and would ask to sleep with the light on, I know the light of God's Word will shine until my fear goes away.

---

* *Who knows whether you have come to the kingdom for such a time as this?* (Esther 4:14, NKJV)

In 1 John 4:18, we read that "perfect love casts out fear" (NKJV). So when I'm afraid, I recall that God loves me perfectly and that nothing—not even the hardest circumstance—will enter my life until it first goes through His loving hands. The light of that truth comforts me.

Now it's your turn. It's your time. Who knows what you'll face in the days ahead, or what cause God will stir you to embrace. Don't lose sight of God's hand and His heart, for no matter your age or where you are in life, He has a purpose for you. Yield to His will and see what He will do.

Turn on the light!

✳ **Send Up a Message:** Heavenly Father, make me sensitive to Your direction in these troubled days. Give me insight, faith, and courage to obey You. Amen.

✳ **Text Helps:** In times like these, you desperately need the Word of God! Truth like this:

PSALM 18:2-3—The LORD is my rock, my fortress and my deliverer; my God is my rock, in whom I take refuge. He is my shield and the horn of my salvation, my stronghold. I call to the LORD, who is worthy of praise, and I am saved from my enemies.

PSALM 37:39-40—The salvation of the righteous comes from the LORD; he is their stronghold in time of trouble. The LORD helps them and delivers them; he delivers them from the wicked and saves them, because they take refuge in him.

PSALM 46:1-2—God is our refuge and strength, an ever-present help in trouble. Therefore we will not fear.

ISAIAH 41:10—Do not fear, for I am with you; do not be dismayed, for I am your God. I will strengthen you and help you; I will uphold you with my righteous right hand.

HEBREWS 13:5-6—God has said, "Never will I leave you; never will I forsake you." So we say with confidence, "The Lord is my helper; I will not be afraid. What can man do to me?"

✻ **Your Turn:** Write or text a message back to God about your life, what you read, or a request on your heart:

_____

_____

_____

_____

_____

LOL

10 Ways to Cheer Up Those Who Are Hurting or Ill

1. *Spend time with them.* People who are sick or hurting are often bored and lonely. Bring something to share. Be sensitive to time if a person is very sick, but otherwise, bring something to work on or share together—a game, a DVD, a scrapbook—whatever you think will lift his or her spirits.

2. *Be a good listener.* People in pain sometimes want to share what they're going through. But don't pry. Let a person talk about his or her fears or concerns without interrupting, and don't offer advice unless it's sought. Remember, the visit isn't about you or your agenda.

3. *Cook a meal or bring them a snack.* Some people will appreciate a meal or treat for the freezer that they can eat later. Others enjoy sharing something simple with you right away.

4. *Be creative.* Use your gifts to create a card, write a poem, or make a colorful flower arrangement for people who are ill. Bring something that will comfort them as well as cheer them up—perhaps a colorful quilt or a soft stuffed animal. If your budget allows, fill a simple or decorative basket with goodies, such as a joke book or devotional, fragrant hand lotion, healthy snacks, or pretty stationery.

5. *Bring age-appropriate reading material or music.* Consider a person's interests, if you know what they are. Bring something fun, such as recent decorating or hobby magazines, as well as spiritual resources, including encouraging books. Get an inexpensive MP3 player and load it with cheerful and comforting songs.

6. *Run an errand or meet another immediate need.* If a person can't leave the house, there may be something you can do to help—run to the grocery store, pick up something, or drop something off. People who are depressed may not know what they need. Simply be alert to what may help.

7. *Refrain from commenting on their appearance.* People who are ill already know they don't look their best. Comment on the things that are unchanging—a person's sweet smile, courageous spirit, or some other strength. However, be prepared to help with appearance needs, such as brushing a person's hair or running warm bath water.

8. *Encourage them with the Word, but be discerning.* Speak scriptures as a natural outgrowth of who you are in Christ—your testimony—but don't preach or try to "fix" people. Allow the Holy Spirit to work through your acts of love.

9. *Pray.* Ask, "Is there something you would like me to pray specifically about for you?" Even people who are afraid to enter into prayer themselves appreciate a simple and sincere prayer.

10. *Be cheerful, yet sensitive.* "Rejoice with those who rejoice, and weep with those who weep" (Romans 12:15, NKJV). Offer sympathy or deep concern, if you sense that will help; but on the whole, try to keep your interactions positive.

---

1. "1977: Hundreds Dead in Tenerife Plane Crash," On This Day, *BBC News*, http://news.bbc.co.uk/onthisday/hi/dates/stories/march/27/newsid_2531000/2531063.stm.

Worthy of Trust

Text Message: *Gr8 is Ur fthflns.* *

My [Dawn's] husband was in the Philippines on a missions outreach in the 1980s during a major political coup. When a military tank swung its turret to point toward the mission compound, Bob scurried to pack one small bag for a quick exit over the mountains into the jungle.

After the coup, when Bob returned home, I asked him, "What did you pack?"

I expected him to say, "My Bible" or even "a clean change of clothes," but no, my extremely practical husband replied, "Toilet paper!"

The toilet-paper scenario was the only funny thing about my husband's crisis. He tried calling the American embassy for help, only to be told that it was up to his sponsoring missions group to get him out of the country. I fervently prayed—more from fear than trust—until the Lord spoke comforting words to my worried heart: "Your husband is entirely safe until I call him home."

God kept Bob safe through the massive civil disobedience protests and the eventual leadership change in the Philippines. And we both rejoiced when he returned home, three days later, to San Diego.

The sense of God's faithful care was tangible in my time of need during this crisis. I repeated one verse for days: "You will keep him in perfect peace, whose mind is stayed on You, because he trusts in You" (Isaiah 26:3, NKJV).

We can trust God's faithfulness, knowing that He will take care of us in every situation. We can trust God's wisdom, knowing that He will give us guidance in tough decisions. We can trust God's love, knowing that He

---

* *Great is Your faithfulness.* (Lamentations 3:23, NKJV)

has our best interests at heart. We can trust God's provision, knowing that He is always good to His children. We can trust His mercy and compassion, for they are new every morning (Lamentations 3:22-23). Every day, in every way, God is worthy of our trust.

❋ **Send Up a Message:** Father, I know that when all my props are knocked away, or when tough circumstances come to steal my peace, I can turn to You, my faithful God. Amen.

❋ **Text Helps:** We all trust something or someone, but things and people can let us down. Only the Lord is completely trustworthy. These verses remind us that He is faithful.

PROVERBS 3:5-6—Trust in the LORD with all your heart and lean not on your own understanding; in all your ways acknowledge him, and he will make your paths straight.

ISAIAH 26:3—You will keep in perfect peace him whose mind is steadfast, because he trusts in you.

LAMENTATIONS 3:22-23—Because of the LORD's great love we are not consumed, for his compassions never fail. They are new every morning; great is your faithfulness.

ROMANS 8:28—We know that in all things God works for the good of those who love him, who have been called according to his purpose.

❋ **Your Turn:** Write or text a message back to God about your life, what you read, or a request on your heart:

_____

_____

_____

_____

_____

_____

_____

LOL

Hurry! I Need a Hug!

Author Sandra Aldrich tells a story about the importance of hugs:

Occasionally, my daughter, Holly, speaks with me at mother-daughter banquets. Here's one of her stories: "Mom is always ready with a hug. Even when I was little, she was a great one for hugs. Back then, I'd most likely be heading toward something she didn't want me to get into, so she'd say, 'Hurry, hurry! I need a hug!' And then she'd hold out her arms.

"Well, I was just a toddler, and I didn't know what would happen if I didn't hurry and give her a hug. Would she explode or something? So I'd rush to her arms and feel proud that once again I had stopped a possible explosion."[1]

---

1. Sandra Aldrich, personal story shared with authors. Used by permission.

911

Text Message: *I cry aloud 2 t Lord & He nswrs.**

It happened again. A ministry couple called it quits—a couple with the phone numbers, personal e-mail addresses, and cell-phone numbers of a host of marriage and family experts in their Rolodex. They didn't even call for help. Why? They were too embarrassed to admit that things weren't going so well in their marriage. They didn't want anyone to know they were struggling. Now the whole wide world knows their marriage is over. It makes no sense. So if this isn't the way to handle marriage struggles, what is? Here are a few helpful guidelines:

Get honest. Own it. Declare to yourself and your spouse that things aren't right. Own your issues and your personal contributions to the state of your marriage. Together, discuss options for tackling the obstacles you face. We [Pam and Bill] encourage couples in crisis to "layer in love" using the rest of the tools on this list.

Get a mentor couple to meet with regularly. Find a couple who overcame the same struggles you're having—financial problems, infidelity, poor communication, addictions, whatever. Many couples have made it through to the other side of marital problems, finding their way back to love and creating happiness again. So can you, with help! If you don't know of any, contact your pastor, your extended family members, or your friendship circle.

Get professional help. Ask a pastor for an appointment to discuss your marital issues. Some are excellent counselors, and the ones who don't feel gifted in that area often know a great counselor they can refer you to. Other ways to find a good professional is to contact Focus on the Family or one of the national Christian counseling associations that lists

---

* *I cry aloud to the LORD, and He answers me from His holy mountain.* (Psalm 3:4, HCSB)

professional Christian counselors by geographical location.[1] Ask at your local Christian bookstore, too; it can often be a good resource for finding quality Christian counselors.

Get some resources. Invest in books, CDs, and DVDs on marriage. Your marriage may not be working because you lack tools. You go to driving school before you get a license to drive a car, so isn't it wise to get some education to run your relationship? If you climbed into an F-14 fighter jet, chances are most of you wouldn't have a clue what to do. But if you first enlist in flight training, then you'll be fine in the cockpit. Likewise, love works better with good training.

Get in a group. Small-group Bible studies for married couples or marital intensives in small-group settings can help you form friendships with couples who believe in working things out. Often when a marriage is in crisis, one or both partners begin to spend time with single friends who can't understand or offer help or divorced friends who might have a negative attitude. Choose to invest your time with people who will provide the support and encouragement you and your spouse need to strengthen your marriage.

Get new habits. Look for your mate's positive traits and compliment him or her. Be nice. Treat your spouse like company. Create a weekly date night.

Get on your knees. Pray together daily. Bill and I have never seen a couple divorce who prays together regularly. Cry out to God. He hears, and He will answer.

❋ **Send Up a Message:** Lord, help me set aside my pride for the sake of love. Amen.

❋ **Text Helps:** Sometimes we mull our problems over and over in our minds, but we don't bring the only Person into the situation who knows both our circumstances and our hearts—the Lord! The following verses prove the psalmist knew that God is always waiting for our cries for help. What is your cry today?

PSALM 18:6—In my distress I called to the LORD; I cried to my God for help. From his temple he heard my voice; my cry came before him, into his ears.

PSALM 27:7—Hear my voice when I call, O LORD; be merciful to me and answer me.

PSALM 28:2—Hear my cry for mercy as I call to you for help, as I lift up my hands toward your Most Holy Place.

PSALM 50:15—[God says,] "Call upon me in the day of trouble; I will deliver you, and you will honor me."

❊ **Your Turn:** Write or text a message back to God about your life, what you read, or a request on your heart:

_____

_____

_____

_____

LOL

Mom's Bad Day!

Leslie Vernick, author of *How to Live Right When Your Life Goes Wrong*, shares this personal story:

When my son was in junior high, I was having a bad day, and I told him I was having PMS and not to bother me. He cringed, covered his ears, and said, "Don't tell me that!"

I said, "Why? What do you think it means?"

He replied that the boys in school had told him it meant "Past Missing Sex," and he didn't want to know about it![2]

---

1. For information on Christian counselors in your area, contact the Focus on the Family Counseling Department at http://listen.family.org/miscdaily/A000000115.cfm; the American Association of Christian Counselors at www.aacc.net/resources/find-a-counselor/; or the National Association of Nouthetic Counselors at www.nanc.org/.
2. Leslie Vernick, personal story shared with authors. Used by permission.

Connecting Dots

Text Message: *C thgs fr Hs prspctve.**

While vacationing in France, my husband and I [Dawn] visited the Eiffel Tower. High atop the tower, joined by Bob's sister, Jan, and her husband, Tom, we viewed the entire city of Paris.

"Look! There's the Louvre," I said. "And there's the National Assembly, and there's the Arch of Triumph." Then, trying to locate and name other sites I knew, I added, "But where's the Eiffel Tower?"

Tom's mouth dropped open. "Dawnie! You're *on* it!" he said.

As everyone around me laughed, my face burned with embarrassment. That was truly a you-can't-see-the-forest-for-the-trees moment.

We often get so focused on specific details that we can't see the big picture. In our attempt to connect the dots of our circumstances, we may miss something more obvious that God is trying to show us.

I lost my "place" at the Eiffel Tower because I was focused somewhere else. I lose my place in this world when I focus on the culture or even my own ambitions instead of on my identity in Christ and my purpose in Him.

Our vision must always be Godward so we can find true perspective as well as God's values. Our financial need isn't about the money; it's about looking to our Provider. Our marital problems aren't about our spouse's hang-ups; they're about learning to model biblical love, respect, and servanthood. Our child with an attitude isn't the enemy; he or she gives us an opportunity to express God's love and discipline for our child's best interests.

---

* *Look up, and be alert to what is going on around Christ—that's where the action is. See things from his perspective.* (Colossians 3:2, MSG)

No matter our circumstances, God has a purpose *behind* each circumstance. We can trust Him because He knows how to connect the scattered dots in our lives. We may not always understand His will or see life from His perspective, but God will conform us to the image of Christ, bringing honor to His name through our faith and obedience.

❋ **Send Up a Message:** Help me connect with You, Father, and see life from Your point of view. Amen.

❋ **Text Helps:** The following verses encourage us to look at life from heaven's point of view.

Psalm 119:18—Open my eyes that I may see wonderful things in your law.

Isaiah 40:28—Do you not know? Have you not heard? The Lord is the everlasting God, the Creator of the ends of the earth. He will not grow tired or weary, and his understanding no one can fathom.

Isaiah 55:8—"My thoughts are not your thoughts, neither are your ways my ways," declares the Lord.

Romans 11:33—Oh, the depth of the riches of the wisdom and knowledge of God! How unsearchable his judgments, and his paths beyond tracing out!

❋ **Your Turn:** Write or text a message back to God about your life, what you read, or a request on your heart:

____

____

____

____

____

____

____

____

____

LOL

Camping with Sherlock Holmes

Sherlock Holmes and his sidekick Dr. Watson go on a camping trip, set up their tent, and fall asleep. Some hours later, Holmes wakes his faithful friend.

"Watson, look up at the sky and tell me what you see."

Watson replies, "I see millions of stars."

Holmes then asks, "What does that tell you?"

Watson ponders for a minute before answering: "Astronomically speaking, it tells me that there are millions of galaxies and potentially billions of planets. . . . Timewise, it appears to be approximately a quarter past three. Theologically, it's evident the Lord is all-powerful and we are small and insignificant. Meteorologically, it seems we will have a beautiful day tomorrow. What does it tell you?"

Holmes is silent for a moment, then speaks. "Watson, you idiot, someone has stolen our tent!"[1]

---

* Adapted from "Elementary, My Dear Watson," BasicJokes, www.basicjokes.com/djoke. php?id=1063 (accessed March 11, 2010). Public domain.

Headache!

Text Message: *Praz b 2 . . . t Fathr of cmpasn & t God of al cmft.* *

As a young mother, whenever my sons did something to frustrate me, I [Dawn] yelled out, "Headache!" It was my not-so-subtle signal that things weren't going well, and everyone had better shape up!

Emotional headaches are one thing; physical headaches are another. A CBS News–*Prevention* magazine poll reported that three out of four Americans claim to suffer from some level of pain,[1] and there are countless reasons.

I recently read about a person who claims to have suffered with an extreme headache every day, every hour, for 18 years.[2] Can you imagine that? No treatment, medication, drug, specialist, or alternative therapy relieved the pain.

After the fall (Genesis 3), Eve probably had headaches for a lot of reasons! She had to deal with physical hardships, emotional ups and downs, difficult relationships, frustrating circumstances, and the tendency to put a personal agenda before intimacy with God. And thanks to her own bad choice, she and all of us women gained the joy of PMS (Genesis 3:16)!

We may be able to change some habits and choices that damage health and cause pain, but sometimes we must simply cling to God's hand and rest in His presence *in the midst* of our pain. Jesus experienced pain, and He cares when we hurt.

Our Father is good, even when it feels like He isn't. Satan wants to

---

* *Praise be to the God and Father of our Lord Jesus Christ, the Father of compassion and the God of all comfort.* (2 Corinthians 1:3)

feed us lies about God's goodness and compassion in our time of weakness (John 8:44), but the cross of Christ, not our circumstances, proves God's loving-kindness.

❋ **Send Up a Message:** I am thankful for Your love, Father. Help me trust You in my times of pain and frustration. Amen.

❋ **Text Helps:** When faced with the headaches of life, choose to focus on God's loving-kindness and goodness. His love will not fail you, no matter what thoughts enter your mind to the contrary. Consider these scriptures:

PSALM 36:7—How priceless is your unfailing love! Both high and low among men find refuge in the shadow of your wings.

JEREMIAH 31:3—The LORD appeared to us in the past, saying: "I have loved you with an everlasting love; I have drawn you with loving-kindness."

ROMANS 8:39—Neither height nor depth, nor anything else in all creation, will be able to separate us from the love of God that is in Christ Jesus our Lord.

1 JOHN 4:8—God is love.

❋ **Your Turn:** Write or text a message back to God about your life, what you read, or a request on your heart:

_____

_____

_____

_____

_____

_____

_____

_____

_____

_____

LOL

Conversations with God

Perhaps there's more to the story of Adam and Eve than we know!

God said to Adam, "I am going to make you a helper, a companion. What would you like your companion to be like?"

Adam replied, "Well, I want someone who is humorous, witty, intelligent, compassionate, caring, loving, trusting, polite, generous, and beautiful."

God paused a moment after Adam's wish list and told Adam that a companion like that "would cost him an arm and a leg."

Adam seemed a little dejected and then brightly replied, "What can I get for a rib?"

Later, God approached Adam and said, "It's time to start populating the earth."

Adam looked confused, so God explained all about the birds and bees. Adam smiled and went off to find Eve. After a little while, he returned to talk to God.

"God," he said, "what's a headache?"[3]

1. CBS News–*Prevention* magazine poll, cited in Debbie Taylor Williams, *If God Is in Control, Why Do I Have a Headache? Bible Lessons for a Woman's Total Health* (Birmingham: New Hope Publishing, 2004), 42.
2. MedHelp posting, "World's Longest Headache—18 Years," January 2, 2008, www.medhelp.org/posts/show/392038 (accessed March 11, 2010).
3. Original source unknown. Adapted from joke posted on MarkThiSpot.com, www.markthispot.com/jokes/adam.htm (accessed March 15, 2010).

Mindless Activity

Text Message: *Mkng th vry mst o th tm.** *

Bailey was a high-octane Jack Russell terrier. To help him release some energy, I [Dawn] would bury the head of a large farmer's shovel in a dirt pile near our house. I had no idea why he loved this old farmer's shovel. Bailey would dig it up, lick the metal, and lug it around the yard, whining the whole time, until I buried the shovel head so he could dig it up all over again.

It made no sense to me. Why repeat a dumb action when there was no real reward? It seemed like such mindless activity—a total waste of time. To Bailey, digging up the shovel *was* the reward, but that's not the point of the analogy.

I used to have a mindless activity of my own. I'd do the same thing over and over when there was no real reward. It was a total waste of time. I'm talking about television. I still watch TV, but I'm sure a lot more discerning. I refuse to waste hour after hour engaged in something so meaningless. What made the difference? Two things. First, the older I get, the more I tend to think in terms of eternity. What will count? What will last? What will make a difference? Second, the more I grab hold of the passion of my life—which is to glorify God, support the saints, and win the world to Jesus—the less time I have for mindless activities.

I [Pam] made the same choice when I worked as a home aid while attending college. My boss watched hour upon endless hour of soap operas, and to me—a woman set on trying to finish her degree and make a better life for herself—all those soap operas began to look the same: Girl wants man, girl schemes to get man, girl gets man, girl tests her man, man fails test, girl wants a new man.

---

* *Making the very most of the time [buying up each opportunity], because the days are evil.*
 (Ephesians 5:16, AMP)

After watching several episodes, I found myself thinking, *I'm never going to watch one of these shows again!* And I haven't. Life is way too short. If I watch meaningless TV, I never get that hour back in my life. It's gone for good.

Do you engage in any mindless activities? Take a moment to think of at least two. God wants you to take time to relax, but pursuing His calling with passion and discipline will automatically change many of your pursuits. Is God calling you to make a change in how you spend your valuable time?

✷ **Send Up a Message:** Lord, I don't want to waste my time. Help me make choices that count for You and for eternity. Amen.

✷ **Text Helps:** We could have made a list of mindless activities for you, but it's better if you ask the Holy Spirit to reveal the area(s) in your life where you may not be choosing the best investments of your time and energy. Though permissible, not everything is beneficial or wise, as the following verses illustrate.

1 CORINTHIANS 10:23—"Everything is permissible"—but not everything is beneficial. "Everything is permissible"—but not everything is constructive.

EPHESIANS 5:15—Be very careful, then, how you live—not as unwise but as wise.

COLOSSIANS 1:10—We pray . . . that you may live a life worthy of the LORD and may please him in every way: bearing fruit in every good work, growing in the knowledge of God.

COLOSSIANS 3:23—Whatever you do, work at it with all your heart, as working for the Lord, not for men.

✷ **Your Turn:** Write or text a message back to God about your life, what you read, or a request on your heart:

_____

_____

_____

_____

LOL

The Problem with Ironing . . .

Moira, sporting two bright red ears, went to her doctor.

Dr. James inquired gently, "What on earth happened to you?"

"Well," Moira answered, "it was like this. I was ironing a shirt, and the telephone rang, but instead of picking up the phone, I accidentally picked up the iron and stuck it to my ear."

"Oh, dear! That's calamitous!" Dr. James exclaimed in disbelief. "But what happened to your other ear?"

"Ten minutes later the same guy called me back again."[1]

---

1. Original source unknown. Adapted from "Ironing Joke," Will and Guy's Funny Jokes, Short Stories, and Amusing Pictures, www.guy-sports.com/humor/videos/funny_ironing_board.htm (accessed March 16, 2010).

Choice Words

Text Message: *B grcus n yr spch.**

One simple word choice can change how we view our entire day as well as how others respond to us. When I [Dawn] stopped using the word *overwhelmed*—as in "I'm so overwhelmed, I feel like a chicken with its head cut off"—and instead substituted the phrase "time challenged," my blood pressure went down and my thoughts cleared. I can deal with a time challenge, but how can I deal with "overwhelmed"?

I made another choice to answer the question "How are you?" with "Great!" instead of "Fine." It really colored my day in a much more positive tone! Janet, a friend in a church I attended as a newlywed, always answered that question with "Excellent!" Her enthusiasm was contagious.

Just a note: I'm not saying you shouldn't be genuine with the people around you. It's important to be real and authentic, but sometimes we can choose to improve our situations by proclaiming a positive response and then walking it out. It's a simple way to make an attitude adjustment.

Mary Kay Ash, who went from being a single mom struggling to make ends meet to a multimillion-dollar business owner, was known to say, "Fake it till you make it." This is what we would encourage you to do: "Speak it, then walk it, and you'll become it." Change your mind. Change your words. Change your life.

The words we speak will impact how we feel, how we are perceived, and how we affect others. Public speakers, pastors, lawyers, and other professionals cultivate a colorful, persuasive vocabulary, but good word choices are a skill everyone can develop. The Scriptures are full of references to the tongue that give insight into word choices. On the positive

---

* *Be gracious in your speech. The goal is to bring out the best in others in a conversation.*
(Colossians 4:6, MSG)

side, we want our words to minister life and grace, to heal, and to encourage others with joy and gladness.

There are also some speaking behaviors to avoid. We grieve the Spirit of God when our words don't edify others (*edify* means "to build up" or "create character growth").[1] We don't want our words to destroy people, cutting them like a sharp razor.

Listen to your words today. What are you saying to others? What are you saying to *yourself*? Choose words that build, encourage, challenge, and motivate. Build someone up today with your words.

❋ **Send Up a Message:** Help me choose my words carefully, Lord, to please You and bless others. Amen.

❋ **Text Helps:** How would you define *gracious speech*? These verses suggest some ways our words can either hurt or bless others.

PSALM 52:2—Your tongue plots destruction; it is like a sharpened razor, you who practice deceit.

PROVERBS 10:11—The mouth of the righteous is a fountain of life.

PROVERBS 12:18, 25—The tongue of the wise brings healing. . . . An anxious heart weighs a man down, but a kind word cheers him up.

PROVERBS 18:21—The tongue has the power of life and death, and those who love it will eat its fruit.

EPHESIANS 4:29—Do not let any unwholesome talk come out of your mouths, but only what is helpful for building others up according to their needs, that it may benefit those who listen.

❋ **Your Turn:** Write or text a message back to God about your life, what you read, or a request on your heart:

_____

_____

_____

_____

_____

LOL

Signs of Misunderstanding

Sometimes, people around the world make mistakes when they translate signs into English. Here are some of our favorites:

On an automatic restroom hand dryer in Germany:
"Do not activate with wet hands."

In a hotel elevator in Paris:
"Please leave your values at the front desk."

On a poster in Sydney:
"Are you an adult that cannot read? If so, we can help."

An advertisement by a Hong Kong dentist:
"Teeth extracted by the latest Methodists."

At a tourist agency in Czechoslovakia:
"Take one of our horse-driven city tours. We guarantee no miscarriages."

At an airline ticket office in Copenhagen:
"We take your bags and send them in all directions."

At a doctor's office in Rome:
"Specialist in women and other diseases."[2]

---

1. *Net Bible*, s.v. "Edification," http://net.bible.org/dictionary.php?word=Edification (accessed March 12, 2010).

2. "Mistranslations We Love," AlphaDictionary.com, www.alphadictionary.com/fun/mistranslation.html (accessed March 12, 2010).

Integrity "Lite"

Text Message: *A strlng rputatn s betr thn strkg it rch.* *

News programs love to expose the hypocritical lifestyles of government, business, and religious leaders. Whether a public figure is "cooking the books" or a well-known pastor is involved in a sexual scandal, people love to hear every salacious detail, and comedians poke fun at their shady character. I [Dawn] listened and joined in the laughter until I heard Christian commentator Cal Thomas talk about the moral consequences of the choices these leaders have made. "Culture once produced gobs of shame for people who engaged in such activities, but no more," he said.[1] It's all about integrity.

Integrity means "complete" (no missing pieces), "upright" (straight), and "innocent" (without blame). Integrity means that we seek to hold on to our moral values—no matter what. In our integrity "lite" culture, it's far too easy to go along with the crowd and laugh at "character flaws" rather than calling sin "sin." It's hard to persuade people that a holy God has certain expectations of His creation when we laugh and poke fun at the fallen instead of taking a stand for righteousness and praying for them.

It should hurt our hearts when we, or others, sin. *Revive Our Hearts* radio teacher Nancy Leigh DeMoss wrote of this struggle with sin in *Holiness: The Heart God Purifies*: "In the light of His holy presence, sins I had minimized or thought I could 'manage' seemed monstrous. . . . I am convinced that periodically every believer needs to be given a fresh glimpse of the corruption of indwelling sin, apart from which the mercy, the grace, and the Cross of Christ cease to be precious in our eyes."[2] We [Pam and Dawn] know firsthand that striving to live with integrity isn't always easy.

---

* *A sterling reputation is better than striking it rich.* (Proverbs 22:1, MSG)

But it's worth the effort! The truth is that those who have died with Christ and now live in Him as believers are not to continue in sinful lifestyles (Romans 6:1-23). We are new creatures in Christ, and we're expected to walk with integrity, purity, and good character. What we choose to do each day determines who we will become.

As Nancy noted, when we laugh too easily at sin, we forget what sin cost our Savior. Christ paid for our sins with His own blood on the cross, and we were raised to newness of life in Him. Our integrity is our gift back to Jesus for His unfathomable gift—His sacrifice for us.

❈ **Send Up a Message:** Lord, help me examine my own integrity instead of pointing fingers at others. Amen.

❈ **Text Helps:** Whom or what do you serve? What guides your choices? Read Romans 6:1-23, which explains that the person who has received Jesus' gift of forgiveness and the indwelling Holy Spirit has a new Master. We are servants of righteousness! Consider these motivating words:

PSALM 119:11—I have hidden your word in my heart that I might
not sin against you.

2 CORINTHIANS 5:17—If anyone is in Christ, he is a new creation;
the old has gone, the new has come!

COLOSSIANS 3:1-5—Since, then, you have been raised with Christ,
set your hearts on things above, where Christ is seated at the
right hand of God. Set your minds on things above, not on
earthly things. For you died, and your life is now hidden with
Christ in God. When Christ, who is your life, appears, then you
also will appear with him in glory. Put to death, therefore, whatever belongs to your earthly nature.

❈ **Your Turn:** Write or text a message back to God about your life, what you read, or a request on your heart:

_____

_____

_____

LOL

A Little Discipline

As new parents we [Pam and Bill] listened to Focus on the Family, read more than 100 parenting books, and surveyed our mentors and friends to try to figure out the best way to discipline our son Brock. We decided that if our child refused to obey and his disobedience placed him or someone else in danger, we would explain to him why he should not repeat the behavior. If he disobeyed again, we would give him a swat on the padded area on his backside. We would give him an opportunity to repent, and then we'd pray with him.

On Thanksgiving, when Brock was two, we visited relatives who lived in an old farmhouse with a wood-burning stove. We told Brock not to run near the stove because he could get burned, or if an ember dislodged, the antique wood home could catch fire. In addition, our hosts had a newborn, so we didn't want Brock to trip and fall into the baby, who was being held in Mom's arms near the stove.

Well, Brock "forgot." He began running round and round near the stove, the baby, and the woodpile. We issued a warning, and yet he persisted, so I took him into the bedroom to explain his punishment. After explaining what he did and why the spanking would happen, I gave him a swat and then prayed with him.

After the "Amen," Brock piped up, "Thanks, Mommy. I needed that!"

1. Cal Thomas, "Sex and the Married Governor," Tribune Media Services, March 12, 2008, www.calthomas.com/index.php?news=2209 (accessed March 12, 2010).
2. Nancy Leigh DeMoss, *Holiness: The Heart God Purifies* (Chicago: Moody Publishers, 2004), 84-85.

Not Too Hard, Not Too Small

Text Message: *Nthng s 2 dfclt 4 U.* *

God cannot sin, but other than that, there is nothing He can't do. I [Dawn] remember a time when my young son Michael asked, "Can God lift a mountain?" I assured him that God could, because He created the mountain in the first place.

Jesus—God the Son—speaks and acts according to the powerful Word of God. We usually remember His miracles—feeding thousands, healing the blind, turning water to wine, raising the dead (Matthew 14:13-21; Mark 10:46-52; John 2:1-11; John 11:1-44). But there are other kinds of miracles. Jesus forgives the most disgusting sinner, restores broken relationships, and redeems desperate circumstances. Nothing is too hard for our Lord.

Our problem with believing that God is *able* to do anything is with our view of Him. Our God is too little, squished into a box of our design. A. W. Tozer wrote, "Since He has at His command all the power in the universe, the Lord God omnipotent can do anything as easily as anything else. All His acts are done without effort."[1] Power and miracles? They're not biggies to God. He can do anything He chooses to do. Nothing is too hard or too impossible for Him (Luke 1:37).

I [Pam] am known for saying, "Show me the size of your God; I will show you the size of your opportunity. Big God, big opportunities."[2]

We may find that we can trust God for healing, help in financial struggles, or answers to heavy-duty prayers but feel we can't "trouble" Him

---

* *I am the* LORD, *the God of all mankind. Is anything too hard for me?* (Jeremiah 32:27)

with the smaller issues of life. Or we may simply forget to turn to Him with mundane concerns. That's sad, because it's an independent spirit that says, "You handle that problem, Lord, but I'll deal with this one on my own." God not only cares about our heaviest burdens; He also cares about the itsy-bitsy details of our lives. He loves us!

Once, when I [Dawn] had very little money even for the necessities of life, I couldn't afford shampoo. I tried washing my hair with a bar of soap, and it left a terrible residue. So I prayed, *Lord, I really do need some nice shampoo. Can you send me some?* The next day, when I was visiting a friend, she asked me, "Can you use some shampoo? I bought this huge bottle at a beauty supply store, and if you can find an empty container, I have plenty to share."

I don't know if God cared about the residue on my hair, but He cared about my simple prayer!

Nothing is too small to bring to Him in prayer, and nothing is too big for Him to handle. Small or large, what is on your heart to talk with God about today?

❄ **Send Up a Message:** Give me a greater vision of Your power, Lord, as I learn to trust You with all my concerns. Amen.

❄ **Text Helps:** Friend, God is powerful beyond your belief. When you get a true picture of His might, you'll never doubt His ability to meet your needs. Consider these scriptures:

GENESIS 18:13-14—The LORD said to Abraham, "Why did Sarah laugh and say, 'Will I really have a child, now that I am old?' Is anything too hard for the LORD? I will return to you at the appointed time next year and Sarah will have a son."

JEREMIAH 32:17—Ah, Sovereign LORD, you have made the heavens and the earth by your great power and outstretched arm. Nothing is too hard for you.

MARK 10:27—Jesus looked at [His disciples] and said, "With man this is impossible, but not with God; all things are possible with God."

❋ **Your Turn:** Write or text a message back to God about your life, what you read, or a request on your heart:

_____

_____

_____

_____

_____

_____

LOL

Lend Me a Hand?

Fear is an emotion to conquer. When we grasp God's power, it helps, but along the way, we can get a little confused about how to apply His power to our lives.

In a children's book, I [Pam] included a story from Kathy Martin. She tells a story about her three-year-old cousin, Mark, who accidently spilled his fruit punch on the floor. He decided to clean up the mess himself and dashed to the back porch to get the mop.

Suddenly Mark realized it was dark outside and became apprehensive about reaching outside the door for the mop. His mother reminded him that Jesus is everywhere—even in the dark.

Mark thought for a minute. Then, putting his face to the door, he said, "Jesus, if you're out there, will you hand me the mop?"[3]

1. A. W. Tozer, *The Knowledge of the Holy* (New York: Harper and Row, 1961), 73.
2. Pam Farrel, *Woman of Confidence: Step into God's Adventure for Your Life* (Eugene, OR: Harvest House, 2009), 27.
3. Kathy Martin, article originally published in *Today's Christian Woman* (January–February 1996), 25; quoted in Pam Farrel, *Celebrate! I Made a Big Decision* (Colorado Springs: Chariot Victor, 2000), 28.

Tenacious Temptation

Text Message: *w t tmptashn He wl lso prvd t wy o escp.**

Morning glories are incredibly persistent. Plant a simple vine, and it will soon cover an entire fence. I [Dawn] thought our two vines had died off in cold weather, but *no-o-o-o-o*. They came back in full force, and then some! I often rip out vines that dare to curl around our tree roses and jasmine, but they always grow back with a vengeance, and under the new growth is a tangle of dead leaves and debris. Here in California's early summer sun, our vines sprout a smattering of funnel-shaped pink-purple flowers, but I read that a lovely blue dawn flower, a South American beauty, can produce 60,000 flowers at the rate of 300 per day![1]

One day, I [Pam] was walking with my mother, a master gardener. As we strolled through my neighborhood, Mom stopped and frantically began to yank a beautiful vine off my neighbors' trees, bushes, and fence line. I was a little panicked, because this wasn't our property, and Mom seemed to be destroying a beautiful vine.

I asked, "Mom, come on. What are you doing?"

She explained that the vine was a white bryony vine, classified as a noxious weed by most state governments because it suffocates and kills whatever it attaches to. Valuable crops, farmland, and beautiful parks have been ravaged by it.

Dawn, my mom, and I are now vigilant in clipping back the vines. God used these tenacious vines in my life and Dawn's to help us understand the temptations we face as believers. Temptations are unrelenting and tenacious. When we think we're safe from them, that's the time to

---

* *With the temptation he [God] will also provide the way of escape, that you may be able to endure it.* (1 Corinthians 10:13, ESV)

beware. The vines of temptation may be beautiful on the surface, but underneath is deadness. We must be aware and *always* guard our hearts (Proverbs 4:23). If we're wise, we won't give our enemy any opportunities to trip us up by allowing temptations to lurk unchecked in our hearts (Ephesians 4:27).

If we don't want sin to take over our lives, we need to wage war against those things that draw us away from God. We must tear down the vines of temptation and look for the way of escape that God always provides. Think about this for a moment. What temptations do you need to uproot today before they take over your life and destroy much of what you hold dear? How can you guard your heart so these "vines" don't wrap themselves around your heart?

❈ **Send Up a Message:** Lord, I don't want to sin. Help me stay on guard against the Enemy's schemes. Amen.

❈ **Text Helps:** These scriptures suggest ways to deal with temptation and sin. Which of these spiritual tools are you using, and which do you need to use more?

PSALM 119:11—I have hidden your word in my heart that I might not sin against you.

GALATIANS 5:16—Live by the Spirit, and you will not gratify the desires of the sinful nature.

EPHESIANS 6:10-12—Be strong in the Lord and in his mighty power. Put on the full armor of God so that you can take your stand against the devil's schemes. For our struggle is not against flesh and blood, but against the rulers, against the authorities, against the powers of this dark world and against the spiritual forces of evil in the heavenly realms.

❈ **Your Turn:** Write or text a message back to God about your life, what you read, or a request on your heart:

_____

_____

_____

_____
_____
_____

LOL

Five Dollars

Pat was riding in a car with her son and five-year-old granddaughter, Sara. The little girl leaned up for a moment from the backseat and hugged her daddy.

Pat said, "You know, Sara, your daddy was mine first. I'm his mommy."

Sara hugged him tighter. "No, he's mine," she said.

Pat shook her head. "He was mine first."

Sara wouldn't agree. Pat thought for a moment. "Would you give him to me for five dollars?"

The car was quiet. Finally, Sara leaned up and whispered in her daddy's ear, "Daddy, I love you. But I'm going to have to take the five dollars."[2]

1. "Morning Glory: Blue Dawn Flower," Flower Expert, www.theflowerexpert.com/content/aboutflowers/tropicalflowers/morning-glory (accessed March 12, 2010).
2. Pat Brumble, personal story shared with authors. Used by permission.

Step by Step

Text Message: *Yr wd is . . . a lt on my pth.* *

With the help of text messaging, Dr. David Nott, a British vascular surgeon, performed a life-saving operation in the Democratic Republic of the Congo on a 16-year-old boy whose arm had been severed. The boy's shoulder was badly infected, and it appeared that he had only a few days to live. The boy's collarbone and shoulder blade needed to be removed, but Dr. Nott had never performed the delicate operation before. So he texted Professor Meirion Thomas at London's Royal Marsden Hospital, who came to the rescue by sending Nott step-by-step surgical instructions via text messages. Nott followed the instructions to the letter, and the teenager recovered fully from his injuries.[1]

God's text, the Bible, rescues us in many ways. God gives us step-by-step directions for leading successful, effective lives. Our hearts are badly infected with sin (our imperfections or our desire to have things our own way), but His Word tells us how to root out the sin, and God heals our minds and hearts.

When we travel in a direction we've never taken before, God's Word is our compass. When we feel there is no hope in our darkness, His text messages in the Bible give us moral light for the next step, and the next, and the next. If we're trying to be the boss of our lives and are heading for disastrous decisions, God's Word can rescue us from ourselves.

God desires to order and direct our steps by His Word so that sin won't control us, and our thoughts will be established (stabilized) in Him. We must be careful to seek His guidance every day.

---

* *Your word is a lamp for my feet and a light on my path.* (Psalm 119:105, HCSB)

❋ **Send Up a Message:** Father, teach me Your Word so I'll know how to walk in Your truth. Amen.

❋ **Text Helps:** Like a flashlight showing the way on a dark night, the Bible is a light to show us God's way in troubling times. Turn the following scriptures into prayers from your heart.

PSALM 23:3—He guides me in paths of righteousness for his name's sake.

PSALM 119:133—Direct my footsteps according to your word; let no sin rule over me.

PROVERBS 3:5-6—Trust in the LORD with all your heart and lean not on your own understanding; in all your ways acknowledge him, and he will make your paths straight.

PROVERBS 16:3, 9—Commit to the LORD whatever you do, and your plans will succeed. . . . In his heart a man plans his course, but the LORD determines his steps.

❋ **Your Turn:** Write or text a message back to God about your life, what you read, or a request on your heart:

_____

_____

_____

_____

_____

_____

LOL

The Ring Bearer's Steps

A little boy was in a relative's wedding. As he was coming down the aisle, he would take two steps, stop, and turn to the crowd (alternating between bride's side and groom's side). While facing the crowd, he would put his hands up like claws and roar loudly.

So it went: step, step, ROAR, step, step, ROAR, all the way down the aisle.

As you can imagine, the crowd was near tears from laughing so hard by the time he reached the front. The little boy, however, was getting more and more distressed from all the laughing, and was also near tears by the time he reached the pulpit.

When asked what he was doing, the child sniffed and said, "I was being the Ring Bear."[2]

1. "Surgeon Saves Boy's Life by Text," *BBC News*, December 3, 2008, http://news.bbc. co.uk/2/hi/health/7761994.stm (accessed March 12, 2010).
2. "Healing through Humor," Miracles of the Heart Ministries, www.linda-schubert.com/ humor.shtml (accessed March 12, 2010).

Reasons, Not Excuses

Text Message: *Mtvs r wghd by th LORD.* *

An old Yiddish proverb says, "If you don't want to do something, one excuse is as good as another." As a young pastor's wife, I [Dawn] counseled a woman who had a long list of excuses for her behavior and bad choices. Finally, when I could take no more, I offered some truth spoken in love. "Those are all reasons—maybe even valid reasons—for why you feel the way you do," I said, "but they aren't excuses for your behavior, because you have the living Holy Spirit dwelling in you, and He can empower you to do what's right."

The woman was stunned. She blinked a few times and then said, "You know, you're absolutely right. They are reasons, not excuses." She still didn't get it!

When we make excuses, we're choosing not to do what we know is right. Perhaps we're motivated by lies, or we have ulterior motives. We may be more concerned about pleasing people than God. We may lack faith or hope. We may be giving in to our emotions instead of living by the truth of Scripture. There may be hundreds of reasons why we make excuses for our wrong choices.

God wants us to *own up* to those reasons. Perhaps some sin needs to be confessed in true repentance, which means turning 180 degrees away from our unhealthy thoughts, actions, or attitudes and heading in the opposite direction (1 John 1:8-9).

Maybe we're making choices that aren't necessarily sin but aren't wise—or the best course of action. The Bible gives us wisdom for that, too: " 'Everything is permissible'—but not everything is constructive" (1 Corinthians 10:23).

---

* *All a man's ways seem innocent to him, but motives are weighed by the* LORD. (Proverbs 16:2)

We can't grow in spiritual maturity as long as we cling to excuses and try to justify our words or behavior. Listen to your conversations. Are you making excuses? Are you blaming others for your personal choices? God *will* help us make good decisions so that our lives will exemplify integrity. So no excuses!

❋ **Send Up a Message:** God, help me see my excuses clearly so I can deal with the real reasons behind my wrong attitudes and actions. Amen.

❋ **Text Helps:** God wants to counsel you, and He wants you to listen to His words. When we read the Bible, we learn how to live as Christ-followers. As you read and "hear" these scriptures, ask God to speak to your heart.
PROVERBS 1:5—Let the wise listen and add to their learning, and let the discerning get guidance.
PROVERBS 12:15—The way of a fool seems right to him, but a wise man listens to advice.
PROVERBS 21:2—All a man's ways seem right to him, but the LORD weighs the heart.

❋ **Your Turn:** Write or text a message back to God about your life, what you read, or a request on your heart:

_____
_____
_____
_____
_____

LOL

Cemetery Celebrations

Lael Arrington, an author who helps people think a little deeper and develop a Christian worldview, shares how kids often get confused over the deeper issues of life:

The first clue that our precocious Zach would grow up to have a superbly wicked sense of humor: When he was 10, we were driving past the local cemetery on Valentine's Day. Many had visited the graves of their loved ones and had decorated them with flowers and balloons.

Looking at several heart-shaped balloons bobbing over tombstones, Zach asked, "Mom, why do people come and put balloons on those graves?"

"Well, because they miss the person who died, and decorating the grave on a special day is a way of expressing their feelings, a way of remembering and not forgetting. It shows how special that person is to them still."

"Oh . . . so they do it to keep their spirits up!"[1]

---

1. Lael Arrington, personal story shared with authors. Used by permission.

Okay, I'll Call!

Text Message: *Thn cll & I will answr;*
or lt me spk thn rply 2 me.*

I [Pam] am always inspired by radical obedience to God. I love meeting people who listen to and obey Jesus, no matter how far out of their comfort zones they feel at the time. We arrived in Canada for a speaking event, and our hosts, Allessandra and Valdir, picked us up at the airport. Within minutes, this Brazilian couple was sharing how they ended up picking us up in Toronto . . . via the USA!

It all began with God sending repeated messages through His Word, through their church leaders, and through traveling speakers who would come to their church and say things like, "God is calling you to a foreign country. Get prepared!"

This was a huge step of faith for a couple who were both well paid professionals: Valdir, an accounts executive, and Allessandra, a math teacher. But they responded in faith, quit their jobs, and prepared the paperwork to travel abroad for missions work. The only foreign country they had a friend in was America. Harry, a friend from a Southern state, had come to Brazil for missions work four years prior, but they hadn't talked to him since that time.

Valdir said, "As I pray, I hear God tell us we need to call Harry and ask if we can live with him when we come to the USA."

Allessandra was uncomfortable with the idea because it had been so long since they had been in touch with Harry. But the more Valdir and Allessandra prayed, the more they felt they needed to phone Harry. Allessandra was the one who spoke English, so she knew she would have to be the one to call, but she kept procrastinating. She felt embarrassed to ask if

---

* *Then call, and I will answer; or let me speak, then reply to me.* (Job 13:22, NASB)

she, her husband, and her son could live with a man they barely knew, for who knew how long, on a tourist visa that wouldn't allow them to work.

One night after a date, Valdir said to his wife, "Tonight. You will make the call tonight!"

Allessandra stood in front of the phone praying, "Lord, You know I do not know how to call and ask Harry if we can live with him. Lord, I am embarrassed. We have always paid our own way in life. This is so humbling. Lord, I don't have the words. But Lord, You know I am willing. I will call Harry. I don't know what to say, but I'll call." As she reached for the phone, it rang. When Allessandra answered, she couldn't believe her ears.

"Hello, this is Harry. The Lord has been impressing on me that I'm to build a home large enough for a family from a foreign country to live and minister here. I believe that couple is you and Valdir. Can you come?"

Amazing! Some years later, Bill and I [Pam] were blessed with the opportunity to minister with Valdir and Allessandra in Canada. Bill and I are still in awe of their faith walk. Wouldn't you love it if people were in awe of how you courageously obey God?

My youngest son once said, "Mom, you have crazy awesome faith." That was the highest compliment I've ever been given.

Be awesome today—obey the whisper of God!

❋ **Send Up a Message:** Lord, help me call to You and obey all You ask of me, even when it's out of my comfort zone. Amen.

❋ **Text Helps:** God told Abraham, "In your seed all the nations of the earth shall be blessed, because you have obeyed My voice" (Genesis 22:18, NASB). Read the following verses and underline the blessings and positive outcomes of obeying God.

DEUTERONOMY 30:9-11—Then the LORD your God will prosper you abundantly in all the work of your hand, in the offspring of your body and in the offspring of your cattle and in the produce of your ground, for the LORD will again rejoice over you for good, just as He rejoiced over your fathers; if you obey the LORD your God to keep His commandments and His statutes which are written in this book of the law, if you turn to the LORD your God with all your heart and soul. For this commandment which I command you today is not too difficult for you, nor is it out of reach. (NASB)

JOHN 14:13-17—[Jesus said,] "Whatever you ask in My name, that I will do, that the Father may be glorified in the Son. If you ask anything in My name, I will do it. If you love Me, keep My commandments. And I will pray the Father, and He will give you another Helper, that He may abide with you forever—the Spirit of truth." (NKJV)

❋ **Your Turn:** Write or text a message back to God about your life, what you read, or a request on your heart:

_____

_____

_____

_____

LOL

Mixed-up Prayers

Author Kendra Smiley shares how easy it is to put your foot in your mouth, even if you're a trained communicator:

My brother was asked to pray before the meal at a very elegant function. He asked the Lord to bless the food and then closed with a request he often repeated.

Unfortunately, on this particular occasion, he didn't get it quite right. Instead of saying "Let us be ever mindful of the needs of others," he prayed "Let us be ever needful of the minds of others." Oops![1]

---

1. Kendra Smiley, personal story shared with authors. Used by permission.

A Skillful Ministry of Words

Text Message: *She opns hr mth n skilfl & gdly Wsdm.* *

Have you ever opened your mouth, spouted something "smart" (by smart, we don't mean "wise"), and then instantly regretted it? Oh my, we have.

After a friend misspoke among a group of ladies, I [Dawn] teased, "Well, *that* was brilliant." When I saw the look of hurt on my friend's face, I clapped my hand over my mouth in shame. I asked her to forgive me in front of the other ladies, but our relationship was never the same.

Women's words truly have the power to bless and encourage people or to crush and destroy them. The woman in Proverbs 31 opened her mouth with skillful, godly wisdom. Her words were like a refreshing, life-giving fountain, flowing with goodness and grace, because her counsel was kind and helpful.

Wouldn't you like to be like that woman, influencing and persuading others for their good and God's glory? Oh how I'm asking God to train my tongue so that will be true in my life!

We must carefully choose what we say—and sometimes just be quiet! But the most important factor is preparing our hearts long *before* we speak. A skillful ministry of words of comfort, healing, affirmation, and counsel flows from a good, godly heart (Luke 6:45) that is saturated with the Word of God and transformed by the mind of Christ.

Once when I spoke to a group of women, I dropped my notes on the floor. They were all mixed up, and I knew I wouldn't be able to get them in order quickly. (I learned to number pages after that!) The Lord helped me finish without the notes, but I felt like I'd failed to communicate. Later, a

---

* *She opens her mouth in skillful and godly Wisdom, and on her tongue is the law of kindness [giving counsel and instruction].* (Proverbs 31:26, AMP)

woman came up to me and said, "You know, when you shared after you dropped your notes, that spoke to me even more, because I saw you in action—making the choice to trust the Lord."

Wonderful words, well spoken, at exactly the right time to bless my heart.

Today, try to use the words God would use—words that build people up, encourage them, help them, or instruct them.

✻ **Send Up a Message:** Lord, teach me how to use words skillfully— sharing Your truth with compassion to encourage others. Amen.

✻ **Text Helps:** If you recorded your words for a week and then heard them played back to you, would you be pleased? Would God? As you read the following scriptures, ask Him to help you guard your tongue.

PROVERBS 31:26—She [the virtuous woman] speaks with wisdom, and faithful instruction is on her tongue.

COLOSSIANS 4:6—Let your conversation be always full of grace, seasoned with salt, so that you may know how to answer everyone.

JAMES 1:26—If anyone considers himself religious and yet does not keep a tight rein on his tongue, he deceives himself and his religion is worthless.

JAMES 3:9-10—With the tongue we praise our Lord and Father, and with it we curse men, who have been made in God's likeness. Out of the same mouth come praise and cursing. My brothers, this should not be.

✻ **Your Turn:** Write or text a message back to God about your life, what you read, or a request on your heart:

_____

_____

_____

_____

_____

LOL

Smart Woman!

No one disputes the power of a woman's words.

Did you hear about the 11 people—ten men and one woman—who were all hanging on to a rope attached to a rescue helicopter? Fearing the rope would break and they all would die, they decided that one person should let go. They started arguing over who that would be.

Finally, the woman shouted "Stop!" and gave an earnest speech.

"I'll give up my life to save you all," she said. "We women are used to giving up things for our husbands and children, and we're used to giving in to men and not receiving anything in return."

Touched by her words, all the men started clapping.[1]

---

1. Adapted from "The Power of Woman," Basic Jokes, www.basicjokes.com/djoke. php?id=566 (accessed March 12, 2010). Public domain.

The Measure of Success

Text Message: *Hmlty & t fr o t Lᴏʀᴅ brg*
*wlth & hnr & lf.**

One Christmas I [Dawn] received an unusual Christmas gift—a pill bottle. Not an ordinary pill bottle but one labeled "Prescription for Success" and filled with motivating quotations. Wouldn't it be wonderful if a simple pill brought success? I'm always torn concerning "success" books. God created us for success, but our human definition and His usually differ. God's definition of success includes faithful obedience to His plans.

Jacob's son Joseph (Genesis 37–50) had a vision of success, but he ended up in prison. From outward appearances, he didn't look successful, but ultimately, what a different story! Because Joseph remained faithful to God from behind prison bars when unjustly accused and forgotten by his so-called friends and relatives, God gave him an opportunity to use his unique giftedness and help out the king of Egypt. In doing so, the king named him second in command of an empire! His success was wrapped up in his faithfulness to God and his commitment to serve Him in love, regardless of his circumstances.

Then there was poor Jeremiah (Jeremiah 1–25). No one listened to his earnest warnings—not even the other prophets! He, too, was tossed into a prison. But Jeremiah was righteous, faithful, and courageous in proclaiming God's message. Lots of other people, less faithful but with more toys and possessions, surrounded him, but Jeremiah is the one who went down in history as God's man. He was a success in God's book.

These days, many people and churches measure success in terms of wealth, prestige, and power. This is far removed from Jesus' example of success. He was rejected by the religious rulers of His day, deserted in

---

* *Humility and the fear of the* Lᴏʀᴅ *bring wealth and honor and life.* (Proverbs 22:4)

His time of crisis, and left to die a humiliating death. He was a failure by human standards, yet Jesus accomplished all that the Father sent Him to do. He rescued and redeemed all of humanity for all generations! Because of His humble faithfulness to the Father's will, we can have eternal life.

What is your definition of success? Does it match the Father's? Write out a sentence or a question that will help you define success from a more heavenly vantage point. For example: I will judge success not by money only but by meaning and making a difference for good.

Now you try:

_____

_____

_____

❋ **Send Up a Message:** Teach me, Father, how to be successful in Your eyes. I want to be faithful and obedient. Amen.

❋ **Text Helps:** Jesus said He came from heaven to do the will of the Father (John 6:38), and because He did, He was a spiritual success. That is how we are successful, too. We read, understand, and obey God's will—revealed in His Word—in verses like these:

JOSHUA 1:7-8—Be strong and very courageous. Be careful to obey all the law my servant Moses gave you; do not turn from it to the right or to the left, that you may be successful wherever you go. Do not let this Book of the Law depart from your mouth; meditate on it day and night, so that you may be careful to do everything written in it. Then you will be prosperous and successful.

PSALM 1:1-3—Blessed is the man who does not walk in the counsel of the wicked or stand in the way of sinners or sit in the seat of mockers. But his delight is in the law of the LORD, and on his law he meditates day and night. He is like a tree planted by streams of water, which yields its fruit in season and whose leaf does not wither. Whatever he does prospers.

PROVERBS 21:21—He who pursues righteousness and love finds life, prosperity and honor.

❋ **Your Turn:** Write or text a message back to God about your life, what you read, or a request on your heart:

_____

_____

_____

_____

_____

_____

L O L

50-50 Partner

A very successful businessman had a meeting with his new son-in-law.

"I love my daughter, and now I welcome you into the family," said the man. "To show you how much we care for you, I'm making you a 50-50 partner in my business. All you have to do is go to the factory every day and learn the operations."

The son-in-law interrupted, "Oh, um, I actually hate factories. Can't stand the noise."

"I see," replied the father-in-law. "Well, then you'll work in the office and take charge of some of the operations."

"I hate office work, too," said the son-in-law. "I can't stand being stuck behind a desk all day."

"Wait a minute," said the father-in-law. "I just made you half-owner of a moneymaking organization, but you don't like factories and won't work in an office. What am I going to do with you?"

"Easy," said the young man. "Buy me out."[1]

---

1. "Ungrateful Son-in-Law," Basic Jokes, www.basicjokes.com/djokc.php?id=815 (accessed March 12, 2010). Public domain.

The Check's in the Mail

Text Message: *Ths wh sk t Lord lk no gd thg.**

Gail's husband, Blair, drove to their condo when tenants complained of plumbing problems. A plumber fixed the problem, though Blair wondered how he'd pay the bill. The next day when they opened their mail, there was a check from their insurance company—a refund, a note said, for a check not previously cashed.

"We had no clue what it was for," Gail said, "but we took it!" After a prayer of thanksgiving, Gail asked Blair, "By the way, how much was the plumbing?"

Suddenly they knew the check, already in the mail, was from God. The bill was $258.35; the surprise check was $259.[1]

Gail said the circumstance reminded her of a famous story about George Müller and his orphanages. At mealtime one day, three hundred orphans stood behind their chairs with bowed heads. Plates, mugs, and spoons were on their tables, but there was no food anywhere. Müller prayed, "Dear God, we thank You for what You are going to give us to eat. Amen."

After the children sat down, a knock came at the door. A baker with three trays of bread said he couldn't sleep the night before. He felt he was supposed to get up at two o'clock and bake for the orphanage. While the children enjoyed their bread, they heard a second knock. A milkman explained that he could not fix his broken cart's wheel until he lightened the load. He asked Müller if he could use some milk—10 full cans of it. Glancing inside and seeing the orphans, he added, "Free of charge, of course."[2]

Dawn and I [Pam] have lists of the miracles of provision we have

---

* *Those who seek the* Lord *lack no good thing.* (Psalm 34:10)

seen God give. I was down to the last $10 for two weeks' worth of groceries. When Bill and I went to the store and checked out with our meager groceries that we knew wouldn't last for a week, let alone two, the clerk announced, "You've won our drawing: two weeks of free groceries!"

We won a drawing neither Bill nor I ever remember entering! I have a scrapbook full of many of the miracles we've seen God do, so when times get tight (like when my husband became ill and was unable to work at his normal level while we had two kids in college), I knew God would make up the difference. He did. He gave those sons scholarships!

Such stories shouldn't seem so miraculous to us. God *wants* to provide and to increase our faith. God wants to provide for *you*. As you pray today, commit one area of need to His care. Then watch to see what He will do.

❀ **Send Up a Message:** Thank You for meeting my needs, Father, sometimes even before I ask! Amen.

❀ **Text Helps:** God provided quail and manna in the desert for the hungry Israelites (Exodus 16:11-15), and He used ravens to bring food to the prophet Elijah (1 Kings 17:2-6). He knows your needs, too. Trust Him today as you read these scriptures:

PSALM 9:10—Those who know your name will trust in you, for you, LORD, have never forsaken those who seek you.

PSALM 111:5—He [the Lord] provides food for those who fear him.

LUKE 12:24—Consider the ravens: They do not sow or reap, they have no storeroom or barn; yet God feeds them. And how much more valuable you are than birds!

PHILIPPIANS 4:19—My God will meet all your needs according to his glorious riches in Christ Jesus.

❀ **Your Turn:** Write or text a message back to God about your life, what you read, or a request on your heart:

_____

_____

_____

_____

LOL

50 Dollars Is 50 Dollars!

Morris and his wife, Esther, went to the state fair every year, and every year Morris would say, "Esther, I'd like to ride in that helicopter."

Esther always replied, "I know, Morris, but that helicopter ride is 50 dollars, and 50 dollars is 50 dollars."

One year Esther and Morris went to the fair, and Morris said, "Esther, I'm 85 years old. If I don't ride that helicopter, I might never get another chance."

To this, Esther replied, "Morris, that helicopter ride is 50 dollars, and 50 dollars is 50 dollars."

The pilot overheard the couple and said, "Folks, I'll make you a deal. I'll take the both of you for a ride. If you can stay quiet for the entire ride and don't say a word, I won't charge you a penny! But if you say one word, it's 50 dollars."

Morris and Esther agreed, and up they went. The pilot did all kinds of fancy maneuvers, but not a word was heard. He did his daredevil tricks over and over again, but still not a word.

When they landed, the pilot turned to Morris and said, "I did everything I could to get you to yell out, but you didn't. I'm impressed!"

Morris replied, "Well, to tell you the truth, I almost said something when Esther fell out, but you know, 50 dollars is 50 dollars!"[3]

---

1. Gail Andrews, personal correspondence with the authors, April 15, 2009. Used by permission.

2. Adapted from Janet and Geoff Benge, *George Müller: The Guardian of Bristol's Orphans* (Seattle: YWAM Publishing, 1999), 166–68.

3. Original source unknown. Quoted in "Morris and His Wife Esther," Warcraft Edit, http://forum.wc3edit.net/entertainment-f36/morris-and-his-wife-esther-t13408.html (accessed March 12, 2010).

Marinating

Text Message: *May my mdtashn b swt 2 Him.* *

One of the simplest ways to add flavor to food, usually meat, is to marinate it. The food becomes a sponge, soaking up the sauce. Most marinades soften or tenderize food so it will absorb the flavors of the sauce. Marinades prepare food for grilling. When heat is added, the marinade imparts new character to the food and more intense flavor.

If we're in too big of a rush to take time to marinate meat for the grill, we may be disappointed with the outcome; the meat may be tough or dry. The *quality* of the marinade will also affect the flavor of the meat, so cooks have to choose carefully.

Some people marinate in all of the "sauces" of pop culture and then wonder why they're disappointed with the outcome. Worldly marinades don't allow godly flavor to come through in our lives. We must be intentional and proactive about the marinade we choose for our minds and hearts.

Do you marinate in the Word of God? Are you like a sponge, soaking up the truth of Scripture? As we meditate (think about and ponder) on the Word, it comforts, instructs, and guides us. But it also makes our hearts tender to the work of the Holy Spirit. God softens our stubbornness and pride so we can yield to His will. Meditating on and memorizing God's Word enables us to store up truth for future needs.

Just as the marinade prepares food for grilling, when the heat of tough circumstances is turned up in our lives, we will likely exhibit the sweet character of Christ when we've spent time "absorbing" the Word of God. We become the kind of people others love to be around, talk with, learn from, and follow.

So, what will you marinate in today?

---

* *May my meditation be sweet to Him; I will be glad in the* Lord. (Psalm 104:34, nkjv)

✳ **Send Up a Message:** Lord, let me soak up the truth of Your Word today! Amen.

✳ **Text Helps:** To meditate on the Word means to mull it over in your mind, to concentrate on what it says, and to think of ways it applies to your life. As you read the following verses, understand that meditation is not a quick glance at scriptures, but rather, a contemplative gaze.

JOSHUA 1:8—Do not let this Book of the Law depart from your mouth; meditate on it day and night, so that you may be careful to do everything written in it. Then you will be prosperous and successful.

PSALM 77:11-12—I will remember the deeds of the LORD; yes, I will remember your miracles of long ago. I will meditate on all your works and consider all your mighty deeds.

PSALM 119:15, 97, 148—I meditate on your precepts and consider your ways. . . . Oh, how I love your law! I meditate on it all day long. . . . My eyes stay open through the watches of the night, that I may meditate on your promises.

✳ **Your Turn:** Write or text a message back to God about your life, what you read, or a request on your heart:

_____

_____

_____

_____

LOL

The Barbecue Routine

When a man volunteers to do the barbecue, usually on a Saturday, the following chain of events is put into motion:

1. The woman buys the food.
2. The woman makes the salad, prepares the vegetables, and makes dessert.

3. The woman prepares the meat for cooking, places it on a tray along with the necessary cooking utensils and sauces, and takes it to the man who is lounging beside the grill.

Here comes the important part:
4. The man places the meat on the grill.

More routine . . .
5 The woman goes inside to organize the plates and cutlery.
6. The woman comes out to tell the man that the meat is burning. He thanks her and asks if she will bring him a beverage while he deals with the situation.

Important again:
7. The man takes the meat off the grill and hands it to the woman.

More routine . . .
8. The woman prepares the plates, salad, bread, utensils, napkins, and sauces and brings them to the table.
9. After eating, the woman clears the table and does the dishes.

And most important of all:
10. Everyone praises the man and thanks him for his cooking efforts.

The man asks the woman how she enjoyed her "night off" and, upon seeing her annoyed reaction, concludes that there's just no pleasing some women.[1]

1. Original source unknown. Adapted from "Aussie Barbecue Joke," Funny Food Jokes, Will and Guy's Funny Jokes, Short Stories, and Amusing Pictures, www.guy-sports. com/humor/jokes/jokes_aussie_barbie.htm (accessed March 12, 2010).

Lemon Vision

Text Message: *4 I no t plns I hv 4 u.**

Deedra Scherm entered the hospital for simple tests but ended up staying five weeks. Occasional bursts of light in one eye signaled a brain dysfunction caused by a blood clot, and the doctors warned Deedra that the clot had a 33 percent fatality rate. Deedra's seven-month pregnancy complicated her condition; both she and her child were in danger. Trusting God's care, Deedra determined that she wouldn't live as a victim of these unexpected circumstances.

"I've always loved that old saying, 'When life gives you lemons, make lemonade!'" she said. She calls it "lemon vision," the eternal perspective that God's plans for His children are always good.

Deedra decided to live a full life in room 489 of the hospital. During the hour she was allowed out of bed each day, she ministered from a wheelchair to others on her floor. She coordinated a magazine exchange program, shared craft projects, and listened with empathy. Soon, doctors requested that she visit discouraged patients and even encourage the nurses.

When Deedra left the hospital with her new baby boy, the blood clot was still intact. She held on to Jeremiah 29:11, believing that God had plans to prosper her and give her hope and a future. Two years later, doctors said the clot was gone.

Deedra returns to the hospital each year to encourage women in crisis pregnancies. "It's a joy for me," she says, "to know that my suffering is now being used for good!"

Her personal ministry, Lemon Vision Productions, provides inspired

---

* *"For I know the plans I have for you," declares the* LORD, *"plans to prosper you and not to harm you, plans to give you hope and a future."* (Jeremiah 29:11)

media for children of all ages, encouraging them to make godly faith-filled choices.[1] Deedra is the perfect role model for that life message, since she chose to make lemonade from her own tough circumstances.

Are you struggling today? Does God have a "lemon vision" for you? Squeeze your circumstances to make lemonade from the lemons life sends your way so you can receive all God wants to give you.

✳ **Send Up a Message:** Father, help me transform the "lemons" in my life into something useful for You. Amen.

✳ **Text Helps:** Sometimes we can't see how God is working behind the scenes. If you have time, read about the life of Joseph (Genesis 37–50), and you'll see that God's purposes are far greater than ours (Genesis 50:20). God used Joseph's difficulties as well as the skills and wisdom He gave Joseph to bless others and bring glory to His name. Consider these scriptures:

PROVERBS 16:4—The LORD works out everything for his own ends.

ROMANS 8:28—We know that in all things God works for the good of those who love him, who have been called according to his purpose.

2 CORINTHIANS 1:3-4—Praise be to the God and Father of our Lord Jesus Christ, the Father of compassion and the God of all comfort, who comforts us in all our troubles, so that we can comfort those in any trouble with the comfort we ourselves have received from God.

✳ **Your Turn:** Write or text a message back to God about your life, what you read, or a request on your heart:

_____

_____

_____

_____

_____

_____

_____

LOL

Midlife State of Mind

I [Pam] run an organization called Seasoned Sisters, and most of us are in that over-40, needing-ginko-because-our-memory-isn't-what-it-was, interesting stage of life. My friend Nancy Sebastian Meyer candidly shares the plight of a midlife mom's mind:

> A few years ago, I noticed coming out of the shower that I had a mild case of athlete's foot. After drying off, I opened our under-sink cabinet and grabbed the Desenex. I noticed after I began spraying my toes that the mist seemed to be clear rather than the white powder it should have been. I chastised myself for not shaking the can but decided to do better the following day rather than repeating the treatment.
>
> The next day I did the exact same thing. Day three, when the spray came out clear again, I finally looked at the can, only to realize I was using Static Guard. Oops! But the athlete's foot did go away![2]

---

1. Explore Deedra Scherm's ministry, Lemon Vision Productions, at www.lemonvision. com. Story used by permission.
2. Nancy Sebastian Meyer, personal story shared with authors. Used by permission.

God Can Use Anything

Text Message: *Nthr r yr wys My wys.* **

When Janet Secor went to the grocery store, her husband, Bob, asked her to pick up a melon, too. God used that melon! At the checkout line, she noticed that her MasterCard was missing from her wallet. "I remembered having it out at home that morning," she said, "so I assumed I'd left it by the computer." On the way home, Janet prayed she'd find it.

Although she usually parks in the street so she won't block her husband's car, that afternoon Janet decided to park in the driveway so she could easily unload her grocery bags. As she opened the back sliding door on her Dodge van, the bag containing the melon tipped over. The melon fell out of the car and rolled down the driveway. Janet pursued the melon, wondering if her neighbors were watching the silly chase. The melon rolled into the street, and Janet grabbed it before it tumbled all the way down the hill. Suddenly she saw something in the mud by the curb. Her MasterCard!

"I must have run over it as I left home," Janet said, "and there it lay until my melon—sent from God, I'm sure—led me back to retrieve it. I looked up at the sky and imagined angels laughing down at me!"

God used a burning bush to get Moses' attention, prescribed trumpets to bring down a city wall, prepared a fish for Jonah as an attitude adjuster, and even spoke through a donkey to confront a prophet's disobedience. The Lord used a runaway melon to help Janet in her time of need. And He once used a pair of scissors to get my [Dawn's] attention.

Shortly after I married Bob, I heard this statement: "A good marriage is like a pair of scissors. Though the two blades often pull in opposite directions, they punish anything that comes between." During a rough

---

* *"Neither are your ways my ways," declares the* Lord. (Isaiah 55:8, esv)

patch of our marriage, I allowed my personal schedule and agenda to interfere with our intimacy.

One day when I felt particularly distant from my husband, I opened my desk and saw a pair of scissors. God used those scissors to remind me that my priorities weren't right. My wrong choices were coming "between" my husband and me to hurt our marriage.

Don't limit God to working through conventional means. Trust Him. He can use anything or anyone to accomplish His will!

❋ **Send Up a Message:** You are creative and powerful, Lord, and I love to see You work! Amen.

❋ **Text Helps:** God can use anyone and anything He pleases to communicate His message of love to our world, or to teach us about Himself. Take comfort in the following verses that remind us we have a mighty, loving God.

JEREMIAH 32:27—I am the LORD, the God of all mankind. Is anything too hard for me?

1 CORINTHIANS 1:27-29—God chose the foolish things of the world to shame the wise; God chose the weak things of the world to shame the strong. He chose the lowly things of this world and the despised things—and the things that are not—to nullify the things that are, so that no one may boast before him.

We mentioned that God has used some unusual things to accomplish His will. Read about them, here:
- Exodus 3:1-3
- Joshua 6:1-5
- Jonah 1:17
- Numbers 22:21-34

❋ **Your Turn:** Write or text a message back to God about your life, what you read, or a request on your heart:

_____

_____

_____

_____

_____

_____

LOL

Not What You Would Expect . . .

Our friend Holly Hanson and her girlfriend Jenny took their children to a church missions fair to expose them to life as a missionary. As they approached one booth at the fair, the missionary stationed there asked, "If you decide to become a missionary when you grow up, where would you like to go?"

Holly's five-year-old, Angela, answered first. "Africa!" she said, with a smile.

Jenny's five-year-old, Travis, spoke up just as quickly—"Jerusalem!"

His four-year-old brother, Trevor, hesitated to answer, so the missionary asked, "And where would *you* like to go, young man?"

With a giant grin, Trevor shouted, "Sea World!"[1]

---

1. Holly Hanson, personal story shared with authors. Used by permission.

Rest from Stress

Text Message: *Ceas strvg & no tht I m God.* *

One of the most stressful days in my [Dawn's] life was during Lamaze-style childbirth with my first son, Robert. My husband dutifully read through the Scriptures to "distract me" while I stared at a huge clock on an ugly gray wall. At one point I wanted to strangle my man! But thankfully, when the drugs kicked in—oh yes, I did take them eventually—I nodded off to blissful sleep. I was virtually unaware that Bob was somewhere in the middle of Psalm 23 saying, "Hey, sweetie. Listen to this!"

Beyond childbirth, everyday stress caused by circumstances, people, and the environment can lead to all sorts of problems—headaches, ulcers, and worse. Some people respond to stressors as challenges; others view the simplest negative situation as a crisis. We all handle stress in different ways—some healthy, some not so healthy. I [Pam] have a few habits that help keep my stress lower even if responsibility and demands are high:

- Before I get out of bed, I tell myself, "Look at the mountain Mover, not the mountain of responsibility."[1]
- Then I review as many names or attributes of God as I can, often doing so by listing them from A to Z in my mind.
- Then I stretch to praise music and roll into my quiet time with Jesus in the Word.
- Later in the day, I'll often prayer-walk with a friend, or swim laps and pray, or listen to praise music in the car as I travel or as I work on my computer or clean house.

I layer the peace of God's Word throughout my day. Regardless of the reason for our stress, the Bible has many antidotes. One of my favorites is Psalm 61:2: "I will cry to You, when my heart is overwhelmed; lead

---

* *Cease striving and know that I am God.* (Psalm 46:10, NASB)

me to the rock that is higher than I" (NKJV). Focusing on the Lord, our strong Rock and Refuge, is the best response when we feel pressured and overwhelmed.

Now it's your turn. What brings rest to your heart, mind, and body? List three antidotes and then try one today!

1. _____
2. _____
3. _____

✳ **Send Up a Message:** Thank You, Father, that when I am stressed or overwhelmed, I find sweet refuge in Your presence and Word. Amen.

✳ **Text Helps:** The following verses are powerful antidotes to stress. Activate them!

PSALM 121:1-3—I lift up my eyes to the hills—where does my help come from? My help comes from the LORD, the Maker of heaven and earth. He will not let your foot slip—he who watches over you will not slumber.

2 CORINTHIANS 4:8-9, 16-18—We are hard pressed on every side, but not crushed; perplexed, but not in despair; persecuted, but not abandoned; struck down, but not destroyed. . . . Therefore we do not lose heart. Though outwardly we are wasting away, yet inwardly we are being renewed day by day. For our light and momentary troubles are achieving for us an eternal glory that far outweighs them all. So we fix our eyes not on what is seen, but on what is unseen. For what is seen is temporary, but what is unseen is eternal.

✳ **Your Turn:** Write or text a message back to God about your life, what you read, or a request on your heart:

_____
_____
_____
_____
_____

LOL

Better Not Said

Did you know that there are a few things a man should never say to a pregnant woman during labor? Here are a few gems:

- "I wish we men could experience the beautiful miracle of childbirth. How did you get so lucky?"
- "You know, this all reminds me of an *I Love Lucy* episode."
- "You want more ice chips? Okay. By the way, did you have time to plan anything for dinner tonight?"
- "If you think this is a pain, let me tell you about the time I broke my elbow playing tennis. That was pain, Baby!"
- "An epidural? Why? You just need to close your eyes, breathe, and enjoy the moment. Rela-a-a-ax."
- "Hey, do you think Junior will arrive before the guys are supposed come over to watch the Super Bowl?"
- "Honey, did you want me to write down *everything* you say during labor for the baby book? Why are you looking at me like that?"[2]

---

1. Personal e-mail from Gloria Stockstill. Used by permission.
2. Based on "Things Not to Say During Childbirth," Jokes 'N Jokes, www.jokesnjokes.net/ funny.jokes.amusing.humor.laughs/Lists/thingnot005.htm (accessed March 16, 2010).

Prime the Pump

Text Message: *Prz t Lᴏʀᴅ, o my sol.**

I [Dawn] remember the day my Grandpa Parks showed me a rusty outdoor pump. "Watch me, Dawnie babe," he said, "I have to prime the pump." He pumped the handle hard, coaxing water to rise from the earth. It was hard work, but his labor was rewarded with cool water on a hot day.

We don't see many farm pumps these days, yet we speak of government "priming the pump" by taking action to stimulate the economy. To prime a pump is to use a strategy to drive something positive to happen.

So it is with gratitude. Sometimes we need to prime the pump of our gratitude by asking questions. What do I have today that I didn't have a year ago? Who are the people in my life that bless me? Where has God allowed me to serve, and how were lives changed as a result? When did I recently see God at work in my life? How did God change my heart . . . my attitudes . . . my thoughts? Why do I love the Lord more today than when I first met Him?

Questions like these bring thoughts to our minds that we can turn into praises. Take a minute to list three blessings you've received in the past year:

1. _____
2. _____
3. _____

David primed his spiritual pump when he exclaimed in Psalm 103, "Praise the Lᴏʀᴅ, O my soul, and forget not all his benefits" (verse 2). David

---

* *Praise the* Lᴏʀᴅ, *O my soul; all my inmost being, praise his holy name.* (Psalm 103:1)

went on to list some of those benefits: forgiveness, healing, redemption, love, compassion, good things, renewed youth, and many other blessings.

These are powerful reasons to praise God, but the apostle Paul invites us to a higher standard. We are simply to rejoice in Christ. Our gratitude is dependent not on what we have or enjoy but on *Who* we have and enjoy—God Himself.

The old spiritual instructs us, "Count your many blessings; name them one by one." Today, on your drive to work, or on an errand, or while taking a walk, thank God for as many things, people, opportunities, and blessings as come to mind. Prime the pump of your heart.

❋ **Send Up a Message:** You have given me so much, Father, but Your greatest gift is Jesus. Thank You. Amen.

❋ **Text Helps:** Psalm 103 is good to read in its entirety, but at least read and reflect on the following verses from that chapter. Read them aloud as praise to our awesome God for the many "benefits" He gives His children!

PSALM 103:1-5, 8-14—Praise the LORD, O my soul; all my inmost being, praise his holy name. Praise the LORD, O my soul, and forget not all his benefits—who forgives all your sins and heals all your diseases, who redeems your life from the pit and crowns you with love and compassion, who satisfies your desires with good things so that your youth is renewed like the eagle's. . . . The LORD is compassionate and gracious, slow to anger, abounding in love. He will not always accuse, nor will he harbor his anger forever; he does not treat us as our sins deserve or repay us according to our iniquities. For as high as the heavens are above the earth, so great is his love for those who fear him; as far as the east is from the west, so far has he removed our transgressions from us. As a father has compassion on his children, so the LORD has compassion on those who fear him; for he knows how we are formed, he remembers that we are dust.

❋ **Your Turn:** Write or text a message back to God about your life, what you read, or a request on your heart:

_____

_____

_____

_____

_____

LOL

Not the News I Wanted

Grandmother Gloria Stockstill tells this story about potty-training adventures with her grandson:

Our young grandson was resisting being potty trained. Although we tried various tactics, nothing worked.

One day he came and sat down near my husband while he was working at his desk. Our grandson had a play phone in his hands. He chattered away to some imaginary person and then stopped and walked over to his grandpa and said, "Paw Paw, it's for you."

My husband took the phone and began to "talk." He did the normal chitchat and then said, "No, we've tried to get him to use the potty, but he's still pooping in his pants."

My grandson toddled over to my husband's desk, looked up at his grandpa, and said, "Paw Paw, you can hang up now."[1]

---

1. Gloria McQueen Stockstill, personal story shared with authors. Used by permission.

God Knows and Cares

Text Message: *Cst al yr nxty n hm bc he crs 4 u.**

God cares about the details of our lives. If we could pull back the veil of heaven, we would see how He is working. Sometimes God gives us a glimpse into His heart.

Bill and Mary Beauvais, missionaries in Gabon, Africa, experienced the economic crisis that gripped this country. The couple struggled to provide the barest essentials for their three children, and one Christmas seemed especially bleak. They grieved when four-year-old Ryan requested only one toy—a small, pink brontosaurus he spied in a three-year-old magazine. The dinosaur was a fast-food kid's-meal item promoting the movie *The Land Before Time*.

As Christmas approached, the missionary couple received a package. Packed 10 months earlier by Jim and Cindy Judge in Illinois, the box included a new mop head and tile grout, clothes for the children, and books—simple, practical items.

On the day before Christmas, when Bill and Mary unpacked the box with gratitude, they were stunned when they reached the bottom. God, who isn't bound by time, prepared a special "impossible" gift for Ryan 10 months before he made his request: a pink plastic brontosaurus.[1]

God sees our circumstances, and in 1 Peter 5:7 we're invited to throw our cares upon His shoulders in prayer, because He cares about us with tender, deep love. Whatever our crushing burden—whether a financial need, a hurting relationship, or a secret struggle—nothing is too hard for the Lord (Jeremiah 32:27), and He wants us to leave our anxious concerns at His feet. He works behind the scenes on our behalf.

Always remember: God knows and cares!

---

* *Cast all your anxiety on him because he cares for you.* (1 Peter 5:7)

✻ **Send Up a Message:** Father God, thank You for caring about every detail of my life. I give You the greatest burden on my heart today. Amen.

✻ **Text Helps:** God has plans far greater than we can imagine. He is working behind the scenes to carry out those purposes and transform your life. The following scriptures remind us that He cares about all the details of our lives.

MATTHEW 6:25-34—Do not worry about your life, what you will eat or drink; or about your body, what you will wear. Is not life more important than food, and the body more important than clothes? Look at the birds of the air; they do not sow or reap or store away in barns, and yet your heavenly Father feeds them. Are you not much more valuable than they? Who of you by worrying can add a single hour to his life? And why do you worry about clothes? See how the lilies of the field grow. They do not labor or spin. Yet I tell you that not even Solomon in all his splendor was dressed like one of these. If that is how God clothes the grass of the field, which is here today and tomorrow is thrown into the fire, will he not much more clothe you, O you of little faith? So do not worry, saying, "What shall we eat?" or "What shall we drink?" or "What shall we wear?" For the pagans run after all these things, and your heavenly Father knows that you need them. But seek first his kingdom and his righteousness, and all these things will be given to you as well. Therefore do not worry about tomorrow, for tomorrow will worry about itself. Each day has enough trouble of its own.

1 PETER 5:7—Cast all your anxiety on him because he cares for you.

✻ **Your Turn:** Write or text a message back to God about your life, what you read, or a request on your heart:

_____

_____

_____

_____

LOL

Reading a Woman

It can be pretty difficult to understand a woman sometimes . . .

Kelly felt a little blue. When her husband, Matt, asked, "What's wrong, honey?" she said, "Oh, nothing."

When a woman says "nothing," what she really means is, "You're supposed to know!"

But Matt did *not* know.

"Oh, okay," he said, thinking the conversation was over. It wasn't.

"Well, don't you even care?" Kelly demanded.

"But you said nothing is wrong."

"If you love me, you're supposed to *know* there's something wrong."

"Now, *how* am I supposed to know that?" Matt asked, perplexed.

"You're supposed to watch for signals and learn to 'read' me."

"Read you?" he said, grinning. "Like a book?"

Kelly *threw* a book!

"Okay, honey, I apologize," Matt replied. "I'm listening now. So tell me, what's wrong?"

"Oh, nothing."[2]

---

1. Based on the article "Prayer That Works: No Toy for Ryan" by Jim Judge, originally published in *Today's Christian* 46, no. 6 (November–December 2008): 11.

2. Original source unknown.

Cultivate Joy

Text Message: *N Yr prsnc s fulns o jy.* *

A wonderful tradition for each New Year is to choose a theme—a character quality to focus on and develop in a family or company. The Farrel family does this, as do my [Dawn's] sister- and brother-in-law, Janice and Tom.

One year, Janice and Tom focused on leadership. Another year, they chose the theme of joy. That was the year I decided to get on board. As I embraced joy for an entire year, I found joy stealers at every turn. I had to be proactive and passionate about joy for it to survive.

Joy is a gift of the Holy Spirit (Galatians 5:22), but it must be cultivated to grow. There are many ways we can cultivate joy. We can celebrate who we are in Christ and the spiritual fruit we bear when we dwell in Him (John 15:1-11). We can determine not to take ourselves too seriously when things don't go the way we planned (Romans 8:28). We can seek the best in and for others, helping *them* find joy (2 Corinthians 1:24). We can learn to appreciate God's strengthening presence in our times of trouble (Nehemiah 8:10; Ecclesiastes 7:14). We can realize how many times our Redeemer has rescued us from our own foolish choices, and we can learn to obey God, regardless of our feelings.

When happiness eludes us in times of suffering, we can still have deep joy because of our identification with the Lord. Jesus is our prime example of joy in suffering—"for the joy that was set before Him," He "endured the cross" and separation from the Father so we could enter into His eternal joy (Hebrews 12:2, NKJV).

Cultivating joy is an adventure, and as I [Pam] like to remind all of my sisters in Christ, "Choosin' joy" is a strong antidote for a stress-filled life!

---

* *You will show me the path of life; in Your presence is fullness of joy; at Your right hand are pleasures forevermore.* (Psalm 16:11, NKJV)

❄ **Send Up a Message:** Thank You, Father, for the gift of joy. Help me appreciate and cultivate it each day. Amen.

❄ **Text Helps:** Joy wells up in our hearts when we know the Lord, but it's also an attitude choice. Think about how you can cultivate joy as you read these verses:

NEHEMIAH 8:10—This day is sacred to our LORD. Do not grieve, for the joy of the LORD is your strength.

I PETER 1:8—Though you have not seen him [Jesus], you love him; and even though you do not see him now, you believe in him and are filled with an inexpressible and glorious joy.

2 CORINTHIANS 1:24—We work with you for your joy, because it is by faith you stand firm.

GALATIANS 5:22-23—The fruit of the Spirit is love, joy, peace, patience, kindness, goodness, faithfulness, gentleness and self-control.

❄ **Your Turn:** Write or text a message back to God about your life, what you read, or a request on your heart:

_____

_____

_____

_____

❄ ❄ ❄

LOL

Caring for Mom

Robin, a caregiver for her mother-in-law, shares this story:

My husband's mother had been a Southern Baptist church secretary for more than 30 years. But for a period of about 8 years, we began to witness her mental decline. As we tried to care for her, Alzheimer's was slowly taking her away from us, robbing her of her memory and social skills. When we could no longer care for her, God ultimately provided a wonderful alternative for her needs in February of that year—a wonderful Jewish nursing home.

Hoping to maintain as much joy and continuity in her life as possible, we would check her out of the nursing home from time to time to give her some connection with the outside world. One December, we wanted her to enjoy the holiday season, but the nursing home didn't celebrate Christmas. So we decided to take her to our church for the Christmas Eve communion service.

Entering the beautifully decorated, dimly lit sanctuary, we joined 300 or so guests sitting in reverent silence while the music played. As the service began, we sat toward the back in case any disruption might arise. To our surprise, the communion service was conducted differently that year. Rather than ushers serving the congregation, passing the communion plates from row to row, the congregation was asked to make their way to the front of the sanctuary to take some bread from the loaves the ministers were holding.

"We'll just take Mother with us," we said as we made our way toward the front.

My husband pinched off his morsel of bread, as did I, while Mother reached over, broke off a massive hunk of bread, and immediately began chowing down, loudly announcing, "Mmm, this is good!"

Snickers could be heard throughout the quiet sanctuary as people tried to squelch their laughter, but it was nothing compared to my husband's comment: "Well, wait until you get to the wine, Mom!"[1]

---

1. Robin Bush, personal story shared with authors. Used by permission.

Ah . . . Satisfied!

Text Message: *He stsfies u w gdnes.* *

"My soul will be satisfied as with fat and rich food" (Psalm 63:5, ESV). Now, I [Dawn] can sink my teeth into that verse, especially if that fat and rich food is chocolate! But I know that rich foods don't satisfy for long. Something within us always wants more, whether it's dessert, a pretty new purse, a new couch, or a new home.

Solomon, blessed with incredible wisdom, wrote the book of Ecclesiastes near the end of his life while searching for what truly satisfies the human soul. He sampled countless delicacies, had great riches and possessions, dabbled with position and power, and indulged his sensual desires with women and sex—the things people think will make them happy and content. But Solomon discovered that life is more than all these things.

God alone gives meaning to the daily routines of life. Without Him, there is no profit to anything. Everything is empty or meaningless— "vanity," according to Ecclesiastes 1:2 (NKJV). But as Solomon discovered, with God at the center of our lives, everything else makes sense. Even our eating, drinking, and working take on new purpose.

Spiritual satisfaction is the reward God gives us as a result of our repentance, trust, and obedience. Repentance simply means to turn 180 degrees and head in the opposite direction. So instead of going our own way, or the way the majority of the world or our peer circle might go, we decide to go God's way. God has put eternity in our hearts (Ecclesiastes 3:11), and apart from Him, everything "under the sun," as Solomon wrote, falls short of bringing true satisfaction. But *in* God, it's a different story. In Him we are loved, delivered, and secure. God satisfies our thirst and hunger for Him with greater revelations of His character and attributes. He meets our

---

* *He [God] satisfies you with goodness.* (Psalm 103:5, HCSB)

needs and blesses us with many gracious gifts. Anything the world offers is hollow compared to the solid satisfaction found in God's unfailing love.

Are you trying to find fulfillment in money, food, friendships, power, a job title, a perfect body, perfect kids, or a perfect home? Ask God to help you turn from things that are temporary to a life filled with eternal purpose and power. Jesus challenged a rich young ruler to let go of his earthly riches and open his hands and heart to receive a relationship with Christ and all the blessings that come with knowing Him (Luke 18:18-24). Today, give something away to show God you want freedom from surface things and are open to receiving more from His Spirit.

Missionary Jim Elliot (who was martyred for his faith) wrote in his journal: "He is no fool who gives what he cannot keep to gain that which he cannot lose." Be smart! Keep what is worth more in the light of eternity.

✳ **Send Up a Message:** Father, fill me with Yourself—Your holiness and love. Amen.

✳ **Text Helps:** As you read the following verses, thank God that He knows your needs and cares about you too much to allow you to place your confidence in temporal things. Remember that only God truly satisfies the longing soul.

PSALM 17:15—In righteousness I will see your face; when I awake, I will be satisfied with seeing your likeness.

PSALM 90:14—Satisfy us in the morning with your unfailing love, that we may sing for joy and be glad all our days.

PSALM 91:16—With long life will I [God] satisfy him and show him my salvation.

✳ **Your Turn:** Write or text a message back to God about your life, what you read, or a request on your heart:

_____

_____

_____

_____

_____

LOL

The Suitcase

There once was a rich man who was near death. He was very grieved because he had worked so hard for his money, and he wanted to be able to take it with him to heaven. So he began to pray that he might be able to take some of his wealth with him.

An angel hears his plea and appears to him. "Sorry, but you can't take your wealth with you."

The man implores the angel to speak to God to see if He might bend the rules.

As the man continues to pray that his wealth could follow him, the angel reappears and informs him that God has decided to allow him to take one suitcase with him. Overjoyed, the man gathers his largest suitcase and fills it with pure gold bars and places it beside his bed.

Soon afterward, the man dies and shows up at the Gates of Heaven to greet Saint Peter. Seeing the suitcase, Peter says, "Hold on, you can't bring that in here!"

The man explains to him that he has permission and asks him to verify his story with the Lord. Sure enough, Peter checks and comes back saying, "You're right. You are allowed one carry-on bag, but I'm supposed to check its contents before letting it through."

Peter opens the suitcase to inspect the worldly items that the man found too precious to leave behind and exclaims, "You brought pavement?!"[1]

---

1. Original source unknown. Adapted from Funny Stuff Central, www.funny-stuff-central.com/heaven.php (accessed March 16, 2010).

Conquering the Control Freak

Text Message: *I wl nstrct u & shw u t wy 2 go.* *

While the ladies in my [Dawn's] Sunday school class prayed in pairs for classmates' requests, God spoke to my heart about a change of plans. *Lord, I don't understand,* I prayed. *Why don't You want me to teach this lesson?*

Julie, my prayer partner, sensed my struggle. She asked God to give me wisdom and peace. Minutes later, I opened the lesson with prayer, but I couldn't continue except to again ask God for clear direction.

When I opened my eyes, I flipped opened my Bible, and my eyes came to rest on these words: "A man's heart plans his way, but the LORD directs his steps" (Proverbs 16:9, NKJV). Receiving this surprising confirmation, I still had no idea what to share. *You've got to tell me what to do,* I prayed silently as the ladies waited.

Ephesians chapter 5 came to mind. *Lord, I have no idea what's in Ephesians 5. I only know what's in chapter 6!* I turned to chapter 5 in my Bible. Scanning the chapter, I realized the first 21 verses were perfect for the class at that time. I rejoiced as God gave me direction, words, and relevant illustrations. But the *real* lesson, I believe, was for me. I'm a control freak when it comes to public speaking. I normally cling to extensive notes. Later, my husband reminded me that I asked God months before to help me be more spontaneous in speaking.

I [Pam] had the same experience in Georgia. I have a set of messages I do for my book *Woman of Influence.* Each example of a real woman has been thoroughly researched and worded for maximum impact, and I'm comfortable with the predictable, well-processed words. However, in the middle of a message to more than 1,000 women, I felt God tell me—a recovering control freak—to use a story of a woman I'd just met

---

* *I [the Lord] will instruct you and show you the way to go.* (Psalm 32:8, HCSB)

in the Los Angeles area who had just started a ministry to women to help them come out of prostitution and exotic dancing. I'd never told the story before. In my mind, I thought, *Are You kidding, God? Talk about prostitution in this proper Southern megachurch?* But I reluctantly obeyed.

After the message, a young woman came to me and said, "A friend in college invited me to this Bible study. Each week, it's so hard to come. See, I just quit my job as an exotic dancer, and I felt so out of place among all these women who seem so perfect. But today when you shared that story, I realized that all these women just want to love me and help me."

Are you a control freak in some area—with your kids, your spouse, or your home, at work, with your extended family? Are you afraid you can't let go? The Lord who made you wants to use you in ways you might never imagine. Ask Him to conquer the control freak in you. Today, practice turning something in your life over to God.

❋ **Send Up a Message:** Father, teach me to follow and obey You. Your ways are best. Amen.

❋ **Text Helps:** The point of conquering the control freak in us is surrendering our hearts to God, and that may have to happen several times a day! Be alert to the surrendered heart in these verses:

PSALM 25:4-5—Show me your ways, O LORD, teach me your paths; guide me in your truth and teach me, for you are God my Savior, and my hope is in you all day long.

PSALM 143:8—Let the morning bring me word of your unfailing love, for I have put my trust in you. Show me the way I should go, for to you I lift up my soul.

PROVERBS 16:9—In his heart a man plans his course, but the LORD determines his steps.

❋ **Your Turn:** Write or text a message back to God about your life, what you read, or a request on your heart:

_____

_____

_____

_____

_____

_____

LOL

Control Freak

I [Pam] once said, "I'd start Control Freaks Anonymous, but the trouble is, we'd all want to be in charge!"

You know, there are some things we just can't control. Age is one of them . . .

Little Johnny asked his grandma how old she was. Grandma answered, "Thirty-nine and holding."

Johnny thought for a moment, and then said, "And how old would you be if you let go?"[1]

---

1. Original source unknown. Quoted in "Grandma's Age," Wallace Ministries, www.wallaceministries.com/Humor.html (accessed March 16, 2010).

Just Call Me

Text Message: *Cl 2 me & I wl answr u.* *

We all need close relationships, and one of the great pleasures in life is talking to friends. God's plan for His family is that we share in the joys and sorrows, celebrations and hurts of daily living. Our friendships reveal who we are and what is important to us, so we must choose our friends carefully and take time to invest in their lives.

The Bible tells us that if we want to have friends, we must act in friendly ways (Proverbs 18:24, KJV). But even if we didn't have one single earthly friend, there is one Friend in our corner 24/7—Jesus! He is the truest Friend, who steps in when everyone else leaves.

Most of our friendships from childhood fade away before adulthood; even many adult friendships don't last. But Jesus, this marvelous Friend of sinners, Friend to all of us imperfect people, wants to be intimately involved in every detail of our lives, every single day.

Do you have a problem? God invites you to call out to Him in prayer, because He wants to tell you great and wondrous things that you might never figure out on your own. What a privilege it is to talk to Him and unload our deepest concerns. We can talk to Jesus just as we talk to any of our friends—only Jesus has real answers and real help.

When my [Dawn's] son Robert was only one year old, he became ill. When his fever spiked to 104 degrees, he suddenly started convulsing. Terrified, Bob and I rushed him to the hospital. The doctors placed a cloth against my chest, and a mat with cold water flowing through it. Then they laid Robert against the mat. As I held his shivering body, I prayed that the Lord would touch my little boy's body and heal him. The doctors never

---

* *Call to me [God] and I will answer you.* (Jeremiah 33:3, ESV)

did find out why Robert's fever shot so high, but I knew the Lord heard a mother's deep concern. In those frightening hours, Jesus was my very best Friend.

Whatever you're going through, Jesus is the Friend you need, too, and He says, "Just call Me!"

❋ **Send Up a Message:** I'm so glad You are my Friend, Jesus. Help me walk hand in hand with You today. Amen.

❋ **Text Helps:** Unlike earthly friends who may not always understand our hearts, God knows and understands us because He made us. And He's waiting for us to call out for His help.

PSALM 55:16-17—I call to God, and the LORD saves me. Evening, morning and noon I cry out in distress, and he hears my voice.

PSALM 57:2—I cry out to God Most High, to God, who fulfills his purpose for me.

ISAIAH 65:24—Before they call I [the Lord] will answer; while they are still speaking I will hear.

JEREMIAH 33:2-3—This is what the LORD says, he who made the earth, the LORD who formed it and established it—the LORD is his name: "Call to me and I will answer you and tell you great and unsearchable things you do not know."

❋ **Your Turn:** Write or text a message back to God about your life, what you read, or a request on your heart:

_____

_____

_____

_____

_____

_____

_____

LOL

Leave a Message

Ever call a friend only to get her voice mail? How about these voice-mail messages:

> Hi. This is Jeff.
> If you are the phone company, I already sent the money.
> If you are my parents, please send money.
> If you are my financial aid institution, you didn't lend me enough money.
> If you are my friends, you owe me money.
> If you are a female, don't worry, I have plenty of money.

> Hello. I'm not at home right now because I'm out making changes in my life, so leave a message and if I don't call you back, you're probably one of those changes.

> This is you-know-who. We are you-know-where. Leave your you-know-what you-know-when.

---

1. Original source unknown. Quoted in "Funny Answering Machine Messages," SillyMessages.com, www.sillymessages.com/ (accessed March 13, 2010).

Cradled in Thorns

Text Message: *4 U alone, O Lord, mk me dwl n sfty.* *

One spring, as my [Dawn's] five tree roses displayed their fragrant blossoms, my little Jack Russell terrier stood on the retaining wall near the white rose tree, sniffing.

Oh, how cute, I thought. *Bailey's sniffing the roses!*

Nine months later, when I cut back the roses, I discovered the true reason behind his interest. This particular tree is the thorniest of the five, and pruning it is a prickly chore. But that year I found a shocking surprise. Cradled in the arms of the thorny branches, on the woody ball of the tree, was an empty bird's nest. One partial egg shell proved a bird had chosen this thorny home to start a family.

I stared at the nest for some time. "What a place to bring up a baby bird!" I said. "Why would a bird brave the prickling of thorns to build its downy nest here?" But when I remembered my rambunctious Bailey, it made sense. This was a safe place.

I thought about two friends undergoing surgery for brain tumors around that time. Each turned to God in the midst of her emotional and physical pain, and in Him they found peace, rest, and safety. I thought of the biblical Job, stripped of nearly everything but the Lord Himself, yet finding God sufficient.

Often I [Pam] counsel people that the end of a dating relationship they hoped would culminate in marriage, or the job they failed to land, or the house they tried to buy but didn't qualify for might feel like grieving a lost dream, but it could actually be the answer to past prayers for God to bless them.

Often, God fences off opportunities that look good to give you what

---

* *I will lie down and sleep in peace, for you alone, O Lord, make me dwell in safety.* (Psalm 4:8)

is GREAT! Thank God for fences and thorns! Years later, as you see God lead you to His best choice for your marital partner, you'll be thankful God kept you from tying the knot before so you'll enjoy the best now. As God blesses you with a career or ministry opportunity that best matches your gifts and talents, you'll be grateful for the thorn fence that kept you from leaping out too early to grab the initial opportunity. And as your new next-door neighbor becomes your best friend, or the person you lead to Jesus, you'll praise God for the thorn bush blocking the original path to buying that other house.

The trials and difficulties of life don't define us when we choose to see our mighty, all-wise God in the midst of them. Thorns will prick us, but our troublesome circumstances may very well be a place of safety, cradling us in the arms of our caring God.

What is *your* thorny situation? Look for God's loving provision in the midst of the thorns. His love is there, and those thorns may just be God's way of protecting you from some worse fate. Thank Him for the thorns!

❈ **Send Up a Message:** You are my Refuge, Lord; a safe place in times of trouble. Amen.

❈ **Text Helps:** Considering Job's circumstances, his testimony was a strong statement of trust in God. Read Job 19:25-27, and then meditate on these other statements about God's protection:

2 SAMUEL 22:3-4—My God is my rock, in whom I take refuge, my shield and the horn of my salvation. He is my stronghold, my refuge and my savior—from violent men you save me. I call to the LORD, who is worthy of praise, and I am saved from my enemies.

PSALM 57:1—I will take refuge in the shadow of your wings until the disaster has passed.

PSALM 138:7—Though I walk in the midst of trouble, you preserve my life; you stretch out your hand against the anger of my foes, with your right hand you save me.

PROVERBS 18:10—The name of the LORD is a strong tower; the righteous run to it and are safe.

❋ **Your Turn:** Write or text a message back to God about your life, what you read, or a request on your heart:

_____

_____

_____

_____

_____

_____

LOL

10 Things to Do When You Don't Feel Like "LOL"

1. **Be proactive.** Do something you know you've enjoyed in the past that is healthy and good for you: a bubble bath, a walk on the beach, checking out a favorite book from the library, watching a favorite movie, reading a joke book or an online joke page (the clean ones only!).

2. **Be relational.** Call a friend—or your mother! Make a connection with someone you love and who loves you: your husband, son, daughter, mom, dad, sister, brother, in-law, friend, or mentor.

3. **Be productive.** Work! Often, accomplishing something will help you feel better about yourself or life.

4. **Be organized.** Spring cleaning or revamping a drawer or closet can be cathartic. A fresh start can come with fresh, clean surroundings. We know it's hard to believe that cleaning house might make you feel better—but it can!

5. **Be active.** Get off that couch and move! Exercise releases endorphins that will make you feel better after working out.

6. **Be a model.** Do a personal makeover. Go to the mall and request a free makeover at the cosmetic counter of a department store, or invite a friend over and have her mix and match your wardrobe for some new looks.

7. **Be relaxed.** Have a spa day (at a spa or at home). Give yourself a facial, a manicure, and/or a pedicure, or sit in a Jacuzzi. If you have funds, splurge for a massage at a spa or health club.

8. **Be smart.** See a doctor, counselor, member of the clergy, or health professional if you're depressed. Get checked out physically, emotionally, and spiritually to find the root of your depression or grief.

9. **Be a kid.** Enjoy something you used to love: eat a banana split, fly a kite, skate, swim, dance, take the dog for a walk, or curl up with the kitty.

10. **Be reflective.** See if you can trace your blues back to a wrong decision you made—then correct it. Let go of whatever it is that's holding you back. Maybe you need to move yourself out of a toxic dating relationship, tell the truth, or say "I'm sorry." Obedience to God's plan brings more joy than words can express.

Courage for the Journey

Text Message: *By my God I cn leap ov a wal.* *

If you've ever seen *The Princess Diaries* (2001), you know that in the movie, Mia Thermopolis is a teenager who's just found out she has a royal heritage. Eduard Christoff Philippe Gérard Renaldi, Mia's father and the former prince of Genovia, wrote some classic words of wisdom for his daughter, Mia, to read on her 16th birthday:

> Courage is not the absence of fear, but rather the judgment that something else is more important than fear. The brave may not live forever, but the cautious do not live at all. From now on you'll be traveling the road between who you think you are and who you can be. The key is to allow yourself to make the journey.[1]

Those are life-changing words!

I [Dawn] remember when God called me to begin a women's ministry. Like Moses (Exodus 6:12), I argued, "But Lord, I can't speak!" God wouldn't put up with my excuses. He reminded me that He would empower me and mold me into a useable servant. All I had to do was surrender to His calling.

Contemplating what that might entail, I wondered how many opportunities I missed because of my fears and insecurities. How often had I failed to count on God's presence to give me courage? With God, Scripture says, I can conquer any obstacle!

R. G. Lee wrote, "God does not say, 'I will go with you part of the journey.' He says that He will go with you all the way. . . . He says, 'I will

---

* *By you [the Lord] I can run against a troop, and by my God I can leap over a wall.* (Psalm 18:29, ESV)

be with you in the deep waters and they shall not overflow you; and in the fiery furnace, and it shall not burn you; and up the hill, and you will climb it with me; and along the road we will have sweet companionship together.'"[2]

Do you need courage for your journey today? Remember first that God has called you to do great things for Him. That calling will help you choose courage. Remember, too, that God is with you. That makes all the difference!

❋ **Send Up a Message:** Lord, I will follow You wherever You lead. My courage is in You. Amen.

❋ **Text Helps:** Are you afraid? As you learn to fear God (stand in awe with reverence, trusting Him), you'll discover a powerful Source of courage. The following verses can help!

PSALM 18:29-33—With your [God's] help I can advance against a troop; with my God I can scale a wall. As for God, his way is perfect; the word of the LORD is flawless. He is a shield for all who take refuge in him. For who is God besides the LORD? And who is the Rock except our God? It is God who arms me with strength and makes my way perfect. He makes my feet like the feet of a deer; he enables me to stand on the heights.

ISAIAH 41:10—Do not fear, for I am with you; do not be dismayed, for I am your God. I will strengthen you and help you; I will uphold you with my righteous right hand.

ISAIAH 43:2—When you pass through the waters, I [the Lord] will be with you; and when you pass through the rivers, they will not sweep over you. When you walk through the fire, you will not be burned; the flames will not set you ablaze.

❋ **Your Turn:** Write or text a message back to God about your life, what you read, or a request on your heart:

____

____

____

LOL

In the Shadows

My [Pam's] friend Gloria tells her personal story of a camping encounter:

We weren't surprised there were few campers when we drove into the campground. The weather was frigid. Snow lay in mounds along the road and against trees. Most sensible people were home in their warm houses. Our family, avid campers, ignored the cold, pitched our tent, and enjoyed the day.

Along about dark, my husband said, "Okay, everybody. Let's go to the bathroom."

"I don't have to go," I replied.

"Okay, but I'm not going to get out of my sleeping bag to take you later," he warned.

"Fine," I muttered as I watched my family tromp off into the woods to answer the call of nature.

When they returned to camp, we all snuggled into our warm sleeping bags. My husband and children fell asleep, but I couldn't. I had to go to the bathroom!

"Wayne, wake up. Come go with me to the bathroom," I whispered.

"No way. I told you I wasn't going after I got into my sleeping bag. Go outside," he said.

I'm a proper Southern girl. We *do not* do such things! Plus, I had too vivid an imagination to go outside alone. I knew my options, and I didn't like any of them.

Finally I crawled out of my sleeping bag, climbed over everyone, and walked outside. In the faint light of the moon, I could see white mounds of snow but little else.

As I prepared to do what needed to be done, I looked to my right. There in the dark was a black figure. I squinted to see more clearly. A bear!

I jumped up and ran into the tent, stomping on my husband and children. Thank goodness there were no broken legs!

"Wayne! There's a bear out there!" I yelled.

My husband groaned, grabbed the flashlight, and walked out into the darkness. The children and I waited in the tent. No need for all of us to be eaten.

Soon my husband called us to come outside. He shone the flashlight on the "bear." It was a burned-out stump!

My family howled with laughter.

"Well, it looked like a bear to me," I insisted, laughing in spite of myself.[3]

1. *The Princess Diaries*, directed by Garry Marshall (Walt Disney Pictures/Buena Vista Pictures, 2001).

2. R. G. Lee, *Bread from Bellevue Oven* (Murfreesboro, TN: Sword of the Lord Publishers, 1947), 114, quoted in John D. Adams, "The God of the Storms," Union University, R. G. Lee Society of Fellows, www.uu.edu/centers/rglee/fellows/fall98/adams.htm (accessed March 15, 2010).

3. Gloria McQueen Stockstill, personal story shared with authors. Used by permission.

Singled Out

Text Message: *I hv lrnd 2 b cntnt wtevr t crcmstncs.* *

As a young woman, I [Dawn] determined to seek the Lord about His choice for a future spouse—or to find out whether He wanted me to marry at all. God revealed His love to me in the Bible and brought contentment in my singleness, but He never took away my desire to marry.

One April Fools' Day, a Bible teacher challenged me to pray specifics regarding a husband. He assured me that no Scripture-based prayer seeking God's will is wasted. So I decided to pray for a young man, somewhere; and if I wasn't meant to marry, I asked God to apply my "husband prayers" to some young male missionary somewhere, so they wouldn't be wasted.

I asked God to build specific qualities into my future husband's life, and I compiled a list of character qualities I would need as a wife. After adding scriptures to pray and memorize, I stapled the list into a red construction-paper cover and slipped it into my Bible.

I met Bob exactly one year later on April Fools' Day. Bob is wise, patient, godly, and kind—everything I prayed for, and more. To top it off, he's a missionary! God definitely heard my prayers!

God still gives me a taste of singleness when Bob travels on long mission trips. Just as I did as a single woman, I trust the Lord as the ever-present Lover of my soul and my ultimate Provider.

No matter your marital status, the Lord is with you, and He has singled you out as His beloved (Isaiah 43:1). Remember that your happiness doesn't depend on a husband or any other person or thing. Your purpose is to bring glory to God in every circumstance and at every stage of your life.

The first step is a surrendered heart.

---

* *I am not saying this because I am in need, for I have learned to be content whatever the circumstances.* (Philippians 4:11)

❋ **Send Up a Message:** I am totally Yours, Lord, no matter my calling or circumstances. Amen.

❋ **Text Helps:** Whether we're single or married, our attitudes always make a difference. We need hearts that are surrendered, trusting, expectant, grateful, and content. Ask God to search your heart as you read these scriptures.

PSALM 37:4—Delight yourself in the LORD and he will give you the desires of your heart.

PSALM 84:11—No good thing does he [God] withhold from those whose walk is blameless.

1 TIMOTHY 6:6-8—Godliness with contentment is great gain. For we brought nothing into the world, and we can take nothing out of it. But if we have food and clothing, we will be content with that.

❋ **Your Turn:** Write or text a message back to God about your life, what you read, or a request on your heart:

_____

_____

_____

_____

_____

_____

LOL

The End Is Near

Dan knew he was going to inherit a fortune when his sickly father died. He decided that he needed to be with his dream woman to really enjoy it.

One evening, he was at a friend's party where he spotted the most attractive woman he had ever seen. Her natural beauty took his breath away.

"I may look like just an ordinary man," he said as he walked up to her, "but in just a month or two, my father will die, and I'll inherit 20 million dollars."

Impressed, the woman asked for his number.

Three days later, she became his stepmother.[1]

---

1. Original source unknown. Adapted from "Women Are Better Estate Planners Than Men," Florida Dude, January 4, 2008, www.floridadude.com/January2008.html (accessed March 17, 2010).

Ya Gotta Have Friends!

Text Message: *A frnd lvs @ al tms.*

We need friends of many kinds and for many reasons. Some friends are "laughing friends." An early friend, Mary, always helped me [Dawn] see the happy side of life.

My friend Maria is my "learning friend." She opens her mouth in wisdom and shares practical advice. She also provokes me to good works and helps me embrace the character of God.

Kelly is my "listening friend." With her, there's no need for pretense or show. She hears my heart, not just my words. She hears my hurts and weeps with me. I can also brainstorm with her about my vision, dreams, and goals. Kelly is completely trustworthy, rejoicing in my victories and blessings without a shred of envy.

Gail is my "leaning friend," who offers support and practical help and willingly carries my prayer burdens. She also answers my endless computer questions and sends me e-mails with helpful information. (Be careful with your leaning friends; it's so easy to abuse their time.)

Pam, my co-author and mentor, is my "lifting friend," an encouraging cheerleader who helps me see my value and purpose. She gives me hope.

Do you have friends like these? Are there some friendships you need to cultivate?

I [Pam] have learned that no one person can meet all my friendship needs, and I'm a better friend when I don't expect one friend to be my all in all. Like Dawn, I have all kinds of friends—those who make me laugh, who motivate me to work out, who encourage me to shop or rest, and

---

* *A friend loves at all times, and a brother is born for adversity.* (Proverbs 17:17)

who challenge me to think twice before making a decision. I need a broad circle of friends.

Jesus exemplifies *all* of these friendship qualities. Only Jesus can be our all in all. He wants our joy to be full, and He prays for us, encourages us, gives us hope, listens to our hearts, teaches and challenges us, and supports and helps us. Though we need to cultivate earthly friendships, they may fail us. But Jesus never will.

✸ **Send Up a Message:** Thank You for Your friendship, Jesus. Teach me how to be a better friend. Amen.

✸ **Text Helps:** Are you grateful for your friends? We sure are! What a wonder that our God is also our Friend. As you read the following verses, think about the Friend of sinners, Jesus, who loves you!

PSALM 119:63—I am a friend to all who fear you, to all who follow your precepts.

PROVERBS 18:24—There is a friend who sticks closer than a brother.

PROVERBS 27:6, 17—Wounds from a friend can be trusted. . . . As iron sharpens iron, so one man sharpens another.

JOHN 15:13-15—[Jesus said,] "Greater love has no one than this, that he lay down his life for his friends. You are my friends if you do what I command. I no longer call you servants, because a servant does not know his master's business. Instead, I have called you friends, for everything that I learned from my Father I have made known to you."

✸ **Your Turn:** Write or text a message back to God about your life, what you read, or a request on your heart:

_____

_____

_____

_____

LOL

BFF

I [Pam] received a Hallmark greeting card from another over-50 friend that went something like this:

"I hate this time in life when my emotions are up and down and my memory comes and goes, but thank goodness you are always there for me."

Inside:

"Who are you, anyway?"

Be Glad!

Text Message: *B gld-hrtd cntnuly.* *

The movie *Pollyanna* captured the hearts of young girls in the early 1960s. With her innocent charm and infectious spirit, young Pollyanna Whittier (played by Hayley Mills) confronted the bitter attitudes in her aunt Polly's town by always seeking the best in life. I [Dawn] remember how Pollyanna inspired me to stop complaining and embrace a more positive outlook. I [Pam] was inspired by Pollyanna's ability to see the upside of everyone and everything.

In the movie, Pollyanna tells Reverend Ford, "There are eight hundred happy texts. Did you know that?"

When the preacher said he didn't know, Pollyanna replied, "Yes, well, there are. And do you know, my father said that if God took the trouble to tell us *eight hundred times* to be glad and rejoice, He *must* have wanted us to do it."

Pollyanna's father, a missionary, taught her the Glad Game before he died. The goal of the game was to look for the blessing in every circumstance—the silver lining in every cloud.

"You see," Pollyanna said, "when you're hunting for the glad things, you sort of forget the other kind."[1]

People sometimes ridicule a Pollyanna attitude, describing the choice to be happy as wearing "rose-colored glasses." Sure, we're not supposed to be naive as Christians—we need to be realists—but shouldn't Christians be glad? Through the Word of God, we view life through the Father's lens and understand that we have forgiveness, security, peace, life, and joy in Christ.

---

* *Be happy [in your faith] and rejoice and be glad-hearted continually (always).* (1 Thessalonians 5:16, AMP)

It's like going to the optometrist. When the doctor tests your eyes, he puts in various lenses and then asks, "Can you see better now—or with this?" But the Word of God is a superior lens.

So, can you see better with your lens or God's?

The apostle Paul tells us to give thanks in all circumstances, not because of the situation, necessarily, but because God is going to work in us and through our circumstances if we yield to His control and respond in the power of the Holy Spirit.

What is your struggle today? Can you be thankful and glad for God's presence and love? Go ahead, put on those God-colored glasses.

❋ **Send Up a Message:** I rejoice in You, Lord, for You make my heart glad. Amen.

❋ **Text Helps:** As you read the following scriptures, smile big on purpose and say, "Thank You, Lord!" after each one. You have a lot to smile about if you know Jesus as your Savior and Lord!

PSALM 5:11—Let all who take refuge in you be glad; let them ever sing for joy. Spread your protection over them, that those who love your name may rejoice in you.

PSALM 16:11—You have made known to me the path of life; you will fill me with joy in your presence, with eternal pleasures at your right hand.

PSALM 118:24—This is the day the LORD has made; let us rejoice and be glad in it.

PSALM 126:3—The LORD has done great things for us, and we are filled with joy.

❋ **Your Turn:** Write or text a message back to God about your life, what you read, or a request on your heart:

_____

_____

_____

_____

_____

LOL

Laughing Out Laude!

Our friend Maria Keckler, first-generation college graduate, professor, and host of WritingtoServe.net, shared a story from her graduation:

> During my master's degree graduation ceremony, while all the undergraduates were being announced, the honor students were announced first, with their corresponding distinction: cum laude, magna cum laude, or summa cum laude.
>
> My mom leaned over to whisper in my husband Sam's ear, "Wow, the Cumlaude family sure has lots of kids!"[2]

---

1. *Pollyanna,* directed by David Swift (Walt Disney Productions, 1960).
2. Maria Keckler, personal story shared with authors. Used by permission.

Marching to the Beat of Your Own Accordion

Text Message: *We ot 2 oby God rthr thn mn.* *

We [Pam and Bill] often describe our middle son as the one who marches to the beat of a different accordion. Other people refer to themselves as taking "the road less traveled." I [Pam] prefer describing myself as committed to saying "Yes!" to God's exciting individual adventure for my life! Radical obedience can have different faces.

Bill and I decided not to kiss before we got engaged, because God whispered to my heart one day, "Blessed are the pure in heart" (Matthew 5:8). I knew "Thou shalt not kiss" was nowhere in the Bible, but God's Spirit had spoken to my heart, "Pam, because of the dysfunctional addiction to men's attention that I [God] just helped you overcome, you are still vulnerable. Take the high road—well outside the danger zone on this one. Trust Me."

I knew God was right; He knew me. I believed that if I were to kiss the man I loved, I'd very likely slip down the slope right into premarital sex. I hoped Bill was stronger than I was. Out of love for me, Bill agreed to walk the high road with me. We knew we might take some ribbing from my friends (and we did), but God asked me to trust His adventure for my life. I've never regretted that radical obedience.

My friend Jan and her husband, Dr. Doug Kinne, felt God calling them to leave a thriving, well-established, and lucrative private medical practice to serve as medical missionaries in third-world nations. In the book *The Finisher,* Jan described their first night on a medical mission in Guyana as a mix of rats, roaches, and Rice-A-Roni!

---

* *We ought to obey God rather than men.* (Acts 5:29, NKJV)

Just a few years into their new calling, Dr. Kinne, who founded the school of medical missions for YWAM (Youth With A Mission), was diagnosed with cancer, and by the age of 58, he was with Jesus. If he had waited for traditional retirement, he would have missed the happiest, most fulfilling, most productive years of his life. Dr. Kinne was known for saying, "The first half of my life, I made a living. The second half, I made a difference."[1]

For my friend Jill Savage—a talented music teacher—it was a moment of obedience that led her to walk away from a career in education to be a full-time mother. She heard more than once, "What's a smart woman like you doing at home?" As she prayed, God compelled her to create a ministry akin to a "mom's university," and that ministry has grown into Hearts at Home.[2] More than 12,000 mothers each year are encouraged by Hearts at Home conferences, which are run by self-described "professional moms."

Today, be unique. Take the road less traveled—God's!

✳ **Send Up a Message:** Lord, help me listen to Your voice and obey You. Amen.

✳ **Text Helps:** Radical obedience—is that what you want to live out today? Listen to the whispers of God in your heart. These encouraging verses will help you follow Him:

MATTHEW 5:8—Blessed are the pure in heart, for they will see God.

LUKE 11:23—[Jesus said,] "He who is not with me is against me, and he who does not gather with me, scatters."

JOHN 10:27—[Jesus said,] "My sheep listen to my voice; I know them, and they follow me."

✳ **Your Turn:** Write or text a message back to God about your life, what you read, or a request on your heart:

_____

_____

_____

_____

_____

_____

LOL

A Different Standard

We [Pam and Bill] delegate chores to our children so that by the time they are 18, they can handle life. For example, bed making as a preschooler, setting the table in first grade, and putting dishes away in second grade. However, the way they accomplish the goal is sometimes very different from our adult standards.

Once, after Zach had unloaded the dishwasher, Bill went to the cupboard to retrieve a glass. Upon opening the door he noticed that the dishes and glasses were precariously perched, and pulling out even one dish would be like pulling the wrong block in a Jenga game.

He called Zach in. "Zach, what's this?"

Zach replied, "A volcano!"

---

1. Doug Kinne, quoted in Jan Kinne Conway, *The Finisher: A New Path for Your Second Half* (Peoria, AZ: Intermedia Publishing Group, 2009); "Introduction from *The Finisher* by Jan Kinne Conway," Midlife Dimensions, http://midliferetreat.com/index.php?option=com_content&view=article&catid=80%3Aqthe-finisherq-by-jan-kinne-conway&id=10547%3Aintroduction-from-qthe-finisherq-by-jan-kinne-conway&Itemid=144 (accessed March 15, 2010).

2. To learn more about Hearts at Home, visit www.hearts-at-home.org/.

The Truest Mirror

Text Message: *T Kng s nthrald by yr beuty.* *

How do you feel about your mirror?

Wendy, age 5, stumbles in her mommy's heels and frilly party dress. She gazes into the mirror and says, "I'm a princess!" Ten-year-old Wendy sports a bandage on her knee—one minute a princess and the next an Amazon explorer. Fifteen-year-old Wendy sticks out her tongue at the mirror. She pokes at her pudgy waist and pimply face. "Do you like tormenting me, God?" she moans. "How can *anyone* love me?"

Wendy at 20 accents her curves one minute and hides them the next. She goes to a movie with a friend, more comfortable in the dark. No mirrors there. At 30, she experiments at a makeup mirror—a dab of this, a dab of that. But when she catches a glimpse of her body in the closet mirror, she throws a pillow at her reflection. Wendy has little time to primp at 40. She avoids mirrors at all cost but grimaces whenever she sees her image in a grocery-store window.

At 50, Wendy opens her purse, checks her compact mirror, and sighs. "I guess looking okay is just fine!" she says. Sixty-year-old Wendy hangs mirrors all over her house. They reflect the light and bring her joy. She smoothes her simple hairstyle, grins, and blows a kiss.

Finally, at 70, Wendy realizes that the most accurate mirror of her life has been her Creator's eyes. His is the truest mirror—the only mirror that counts.

Do you know how truly beautiful you are? The Father calls His children beautiful, not because they are lovely on the outside, but because they are "in Christ." Believers are beautiful to God simply because He loves them. As we get older, our outer beauty may fade, but a woman

---

* *The king is enthralled by your beauty; honor him, for he is your lord.* (Psalm 45:11)

who respects and obeys God will be praised as truly beautiful (Proverbs 31:30).

We are God's "workmanship" (Ephesians 2:10), wonderfully and skillfully made (Psalm 139:13-16). God is an awesome Artist. He "crowns" (adorns) us with salvation (Psalm 149:4), and His beauty in us transcends all time. In God's eyes, we're all beautiful! YOU are beautiful!

✳ **Send Up a Message:** Father, forgive me when I doubt Your handiwork in creating me. I thank You today for Your creativity and love. Amen.

✳ **Text Helps:** God made you and designed your unique personality. You are His masterpiece. As you read the following verses, stand before the mirror of God's Word and see how much He loves you.

PSALM 139:13-16—You created my inmost being; you knit me together in my mother's womb. I praise you because I am fearfully and wonderfully made; your works are wonderful, I know that full well. My frame was not hidden from you when I was made in the secret place. When I was woven together in the depths of the earth, your eyes saw my unformed body. All the days ordained for me were written in your book before one of them came to be.

PROVERBS 31:30—Charm is deceptive, and beauty is fleeting; but a woman who fears the LORD is to be praised.

1 PETER 3:3-4—Your beauty should not come from outward adornment, such as braided hair and the wearing of gold jewelry and fine clothes. Instead, it should be that of your inner self, the unfading beauty of a gentle and quiet spirit, which is of great worth in God's sight.

✳ **Your Turn:** Write or text a message back to God about your life, what you read, or a request on your heart:

_____

_____

_____

_____

LOL

Face Value

A little boy was fascinated as he watched his mother smooth cold cream on her face.

"Mommy," he asked, "why do you put that stuff on your face?"

"To make myself beautiful," his mother replied as she began removing the cream with a tissue.

"What's the matter?" he asked. "Are you giving up already?"[1]

---

1. Original source unknown. Quoted in "Don't Give Up So Easily, Mom!" Homemaking—Clean Humor, HomeschoolChristian.com www.homeschoolchristian. net/homemaking//cleanhumor/lgms.php (accessed March 15, 2010).

Take Care of Yourself

Text Message: *whtevr 1 soz, tht wl he lso reap.* *

"You know you're getting old," a saying goes, "when your mind makes contracts your body can't keep!"[1]

I [Dawn] wish I knew at 30 what I know now. From the moment we're born, we begin a long journey toward our last breath, and the choices we make along the way will play a big role in how we spend our final days on earth.

Junk food is called that for a reason! Bodies that aren't exercised get flabby. Undisciplined minds and lives will reap few rewards. We somehow think we will be the exception, but what we reap we *will* sow. If we "plant" in foolishness, we will reap the results of foolishness (Proverbs 1:31; Galatians 6:7-9).

Though there are consequences to lax living, there is always hope for change. If you are young, make smart choices *now* and every day that will strengthen you for the days ahead. If you're older, some consequences of aging are inevitable, but examine your life to see what you *can* improve with some simple disciplines and changes. It's worth the effort!

Don't allow Satan to convince you that you're a failure simply because you've made some wrong choices. You have the rest of your life to make wiser ones!

Get back into the great adventure of loving and serving God and others. First, ask God for a fresh vision of His plans for your life. Then take steps to follow His will. Take care of yourself! Eat right. Think right. Act right. *Choose* right.

---

* *Do not be deceived: God is not mocked, for whatever one sows, that will he also reap.* (Galatians 6:7, ESV)

Have fun as you learn to take better care of yourself. What new sport could you learn that would get you moving again? What hobby could help you stretch your mind or creativity? What group could you join to build healthy, encouraging relationships? What could you change—hairdo, fashion, makeup, etc.—that would boost your appearance?

This year, I [Pam] made an appointment with image consultant Jill Swanson, who offers this simple yet profound insight in her book *Simply Beautiful*, "If nothing changes, nothing changes."[2]

Don't give up; you can do whatever God calls you to do through Christ's strength (Philippians 4:13). It might be time for a change. Really, change can be a good thing!

※ **Send Up a Message:** I'm so glad, Lord, that it's never too late to change. Show me how to bring You glory through wise choices. Amen.

※ **Text Helps:** You will make hundreds of small choices today. God can help you make wise ones. Read the following verses and think about the choices you make every day. Do they please God? Are they wise?

PROVERBS 4:5-8—Get wisdom, get understanding; do not forget my words or swerve from them. Do not forsake wisdom, and she will protect you; love her, and she will watch over you. Wisdom is supreme; therefore get wisdom. Though it cost all you have, get understanding. Esteem her, and she will exalt you; embrace her, and she will honor you.

PROVERBS 15:21—Folly delights a man who lacks judgment, but a man of understanding keeps a straight course.

1 CORINTHIANS 15:58; 2 CORINTHIANS 5:10—Always give yourselves fully to the work of the Lord, because you know that your labor in the Lord is not in vain. . . . For we must all appear before the judgment seat of Christ, that each one may receive what is due him for the things done while in the body, whether good or bad.

❄ **Your Turn:** Write or text a message back to God about your life, what you read, or a request on your heart:

_____

_____

_____

_____

_____

_____

LOL

I'm Trying to Remember . . .

Forgetfulness is one of the signs of old age, as this story illustrates:

> Three ladies were discussing the travails of getting older. One said, "Sometimes I catch myself with a jar of mayonnaise in my hand while standing in front of the refrigerator, and I can't remember whether I need to put it away or start making a sandwich."
>
> The second lady chimed in with, "Yes, sometimes I find myself on the landing of the stairs and can't remember whether I was on my way up or on my way down."
>
> The third one responded, "Well, ladies, I'm glad I don't have that problem—knock on wood," as she rapped her knuckles on the table. "That must be the door. I'll get it!"[3]

---

1. Original source unknown. Quoted in "Getting Old When . . .," Aha! Jokes, www.ahajokes.com/age27.html (accessed March 15, 2010).

2. Jill Swanson, *Simply Beautiful: Inside and Out* (Rochester, MN: River City Press, 2005), 107.

3. Original source unknown. Adapted from "I Am Not Forgetful," Aha! Jokes, www.ahajokes.com/age24.html (accessed March 15, 2010).

Navigating Change

Text Message: *Thrfr we wil nt fear tho t erth shld chng . . .**

I [Pam] was sitting in an intensive-care unit, keeping watch with my husband, Bill, over our son. Bill had just ended a job he loved, and our lives had been turned upside down.

I had been asked to endorse a book—*Grace Points* by Jane Rubietta—and as I sat in that hospital room, God sent His hope in the middle of my pain as I read these words: "God is working just beyond the headlights of your life."[1]

Here are a few other things I've learned about navigating change:

1. Stand on the sure when you're dealing with the unsure. In my messages on *Woman of Confidence,*[2] I encourage women to follow the example of Naomi in the book of Ruth, who, when her husband and sons died, went back to the last place she knew she had heard from God: her homeland. If you're feeling lost, go back to familiar people and places—and the promises from God's Word.

2. Concentrate on the certain when dealing with the uncertain. Look at nature, the consistent roll of the waves—tide in, tide out—or the sun that rises and sets each day. God is in control. Psalm 50:6 reminds us, "The heavens proclaim his righteousness." Observe the certain in nature and trust in that same reliable control of God in your own life. God is in control even if you can't see or feel Him, so watch a sunrise or a moonrise today to remind yourself of His power to provide!

3. Do the known while waiting on the unknown. Do what is healthy while you're waiting and wondering. Clean house, get dressed, visit

---

* *Therefore we will not fear, though the earth should change and though the mountains slip into the heart of the sea.* (Psalm 46:2, NASB)

friends, and continue in ministry, even if it's just helping the next person God brings across your path. Proverbs 31:13 gives an example of a woman who "works with eager hands." If you don't have answers to your questions, do some research and then step out to call, write, or visit the people who can help. Function on the thread of information you *do* know, and it will likely lead to a person or resource with more information.

4. Focus on God's faithfulness while waiting on the future. Remember God's faithfulness in your own life. Store away memories of God's faithfulness in a scrapbook, a photo album, and in your heart—like the psalmist who lists 25 faithful victories of God in Psalm 136 and ends each accomplishment with the praise "His love endures forever."

❊ **Send Up a Message:** Lord, when I am navigating change, help me focus on You, not my circumstances. Be the compass needle of my life. Amen.

❊ **Text Helps:** Naomi returned to her family back in Bethlehem—familiar surroundings—when her life fell apart. Read her story in Ruth 1. Then switch gears and rejoice with the psalmist in this beautiful tribute to God's faithful love to Israel.

PSALM 136:1-5—Give thanks to the LORD, for he is good. His love endures forever. Give thanks to the God of gods. His love endures forever. Give thanks to the Lord of lords: His love endures forever. To him who alone does great wonders, His love endures forever. Who by his understanding made the heavens, His love endures forever. . . .

Now look up Psalm 136 in your Bible and underline all the places where the writer reminds us that God's love endures forever!

LAMENTATIONS 3:22-23—Because of the LORD's great love we are not consumed, for his compassions never fail. They are new every morning; great is your faithfulness.

✳ **Your Turn:** Write or text a message back to God about your life, what you read, or a request on your heart:

_____

_____

_____

_____

LOL

Change

Women live with change all their lives. Estrogen, pregnancy, PMS, and menopause affect our lives in significant ways that most men just can't understand. Following are some humorous answers to the questions we might have during pregnancy:

Q: Should I have a baby after 35?

A: No, 35 children are enough.

Q: I'm two months pregnant now. When will my baby move?

A: With any luck, right after college.

Q: My childbirth instructor says it's not pain I'll feel during labor; it's pressure. Is she right?

A: Yes, in the same way that a tornado might be called an air current.

Q: When is the best time to get an epidural?

A: Right after you find out you are pregnant.

Q: Our baby was born last week. When will my wife begin to feel and act normal again?

A: When the kids are in college.[3]

---

1. Jane Rubietta, *Grace Points* (Downers Grove, IL: InterVarsity, 2004).
2. Pam Farrel, *Woman of Confidence: Step into God's Adventure for Your Life* (Eugene, OR: Harvest House, 2009).
3. Original source unknown. Quoted in "So You Wanna Have a Baby . . .," FunPages. com, www.funpages.com/havingababy/ (accessed March 15, 2010).

All I Need and More

Text Message: & *my God wl mt al yr nds accdg 2 hs glrus rchs n CJ.**

When I [Dawn] traveled during the early days of ministry work, funds were scarce. One month, there wasn't enough for a small team allowance, so I asked God to provide for some simple needs—hair spray, nylons, and breath mints. That week, when I arrived at the home where I would stay while ministering at a new church, my hostess led me to my room. Imagine my delight to find a gift basket on my bed, stuffed with *exactly* what I'd prayed for—and so much more. I asked my heavenly Father for "bread," and He didn't give me a "stone" (Matthew 7:9-11).

I [Pam] went through a very hard emotional experience. Our ministry and family transition and responsibilities had me exhausted, yet I needed to travel overseas on a 24-hour flight to minister to military wives sending their spouses off to war. I begged God to replenish me for my next task, and my personal assistant prayed that God would give me a "kiss from heaven" on the flight.

When I checked in at the airport, the American Airlines attendant said, "There's room on this flight, so I've moved you. You'll have an entire row of five seats to spread out and lie down." Heavenly rest!

The Bible is clear that God provides for His children, but we've learned that not every request results in a beautiful gift basket. Godly people still lose jobs, pinch pennies, and suffer in pain. God is in charge of when and how He supplies our needs, but He is honored by our persistent prayers. As we pray, He will send us kisses from heaven and gift baskets of essentials to keep us encouraged and inspired to stay connected to Him.

---

* *My God will meet all your needs according to his glorious riches in Christ Jesus.* (Philippians 4:19)

When heaven seems silent, God may have a greater purpose than we can comprehend. Sometimes He holds back because we are willful, disobedient children who need to repent and change our ways. His answers are always designed to help us remember that He is the Lord. God delays some answers so we'll learn patience and greater dependence on Him; other answers won't come until heaven. Our best prayer is "Your will be done, Lord."

God's ultimate purpose is to develop our character in Christ. When trials come, God stretches our faith, teaches us to trust His promises, and sometimes sends us in a new direction. God clothes the lilies of the field and isn't hindered by the price of gas or groceries. So ask and believe; God loves to give to His children.

Today, God may or may not give the answer to all your requests, but look for a kiss from heaven or His basket of provision along your path. When your eyes and heart are wide open, you'll see His unending supply of love.

❋ **Send Up a Message:** Lord, I open my heart in surrender and my hands to receive from Your rich supply. Amen.

❋ **Text Helps:** Jesus shared a wonderful parable about persistent prayer in Luke 18:1-8. As you read this story, think about your own needs and take them to God in faith. Then read these other confidence builders!

PSALM 23:1—The LORD is my shepherd, I shall not be in want.

PSALM 81:10—Open wide your mouth and I will fill it.

PSALM 84:11—The LORD God is a sun and shield; the LORD bestows favor and honor; no good thing does he withhold from those whose walk is blameless.

MATTHEW 7:9-11—Which of you, if his son asks for bread, will give him a stone? Or if he asks for a fish, will give him a snake? If you, then, though you are evil, know how to give good gifts to your children, how much more will your Father in heaven give good gifts to those who ask him!

❋ **Your Turn:** Write or text a message back to God about your life, what you read, or a request on your heart:

_____

_____

_____

_____

LOL

Flip-Flop

My [Pam's] friend Jeanne Zornes, author of *Spiritual Spandex for the Outstretched Soul*, shared this tongue-tangled laugh:

> With a surgical biopsy on my calendar, I needed to make sure my young family's needs were taken care of in my drowsy aftermath. A couple of days before the appointment, my best friend called.
>
> "Don't you worry," she insisted. "I'll bring your family a meal the evening after your autopsy."
>
> Long pause.
>
> "I hope it doesn't turn out like *that*," I said.[1]

---

1. Jeanne Zornes, personal story shared with Pam. Used by permission.

Who *Are* You?

Text Message: *No 1 nos t Fthr xcpt t Sn.* *

Both of my [Dawn's] sons played basketball and baseball in high school. Both were baseball pitchers, but they had different strength sets in basketball. Robert amazed me with his long shots, way behind the three-point line. Mike's straight-up dunks made my mouth drop open every time.

Though Mike was a baseball star, drafted by the Phillies out of high school, I'll never forget one of his basketball games. Injured in the second quarter, he refused to remain on the bench and nurse his painful, wounded knee and back. Instead, Mike "powered up" and played injured, inspiring the team to victory. They won by 5 points in the fourth overtime! After the game, amazed by his grit and 41 personal points, I hugged Mike and said, "Who *are* you?"

Sometimes as I read God's Word, I feel the same way. I keep seeing amazing, different sides of God—His extraordinary mercy, His boundless love, His concern and kindness, His awesome power. Like a multifaceted diamond, God's true character keeps shining through, but it sparkles in new ways every time I read and meditate on His Word. God reveals Himself not only in creation but also through the sages and prophets of Scripture, and ultimately in His Son, Jesus.

The Father longs for us to know Him. To "know" in the Bible indicates intimacy. The apostle Paul's earnest goal, after his radical conversion, was to know God. That desire motivated and dominated his entire life (Philippians 3:8-10).

Do you want to know more about God? Study the words and ways of

---

* *No one knows the Son except the Father, and no one knows the Father except the Son and anyone to whom the Son desires to reveal Him.* (Matthew 11:27, HCSB)

His Son. Get a journal and, every day, read the Bible, asking God to show you something new about Himself or about life from His perspective.

✸ **Send Up a Message:** Father, reveal Yourself to me as I study Your Word, so I can love You even more. Amen.

✸ **Text Helps:** Read the apostle Paul's powerful statement about wanting to know Christ (Philippians 3:8-10). Is that your heart's desire? The following verses give us a glimpse into who God is:

PSALM 19:1—The heavens declare the glory of God; the skies proclaim the work of his hands.

JOHN 14:9—[Jesus said,] "Anyone who has seen me has seen the Father."

ROMANS 1:20—Since the creation of the world God's invisible qualities—his eternal power and divine nature—have been clearly seen, being understood from what has been made, so that men are without excuse.

1 CORINTHIANS 13:12—Now we see but a poor reflection as in a mirror; then we shall see face to face. Now I know in part; then I shall know fully, even as I am fully known.

✸ **Your Turn:** Write or text a message back to God about your life, what you read, or a request on your heart:

_____

_____

_____

LOL

What Do You Want?

This tip we found on "Stress-Reducing Menu Planning" may just work!

I have changed my system for labeling homemade freezer meals.
I used to carefully note in large clear letters, "Meatloaf" or "Pot Roast"

or "Steak and Vegetables" or "Chicken and Dumplings" or "Beef Pot Pie."

However, I used to get very frustrated when I asked my husband what he wanted for dinner, because he never asked for any of those things. So I decided to stock the freezer with what he really likes.

If you look in my freezer now, you'll see a whole new set of labels. You'll find dinners with neat, legible tags that say: "Whatever," "Anything," "I Don't Know," "I Don't Care," "Something Good," or "Food." My frustration is reduced, because no matter what my husband replies when I ask him what he wants for dinner, I know that it will be there waiting.[1]

---

1. "Stress-Reducing Menu Planning Tip," Bag-O-Laughs, Grant's Graceland, June 6, 2002, www.grantsgraceland.org/bag4/menu.html, (accessed March 15, 2010).

First and Last Words

Text Message: *A mn hs joy n an apt nswr & hw dlghtfl s a timly wrd!**

How we greet each other sets the mood for our time together, and how we depart leaves a lasting impression. I [Pam] have made it a habit of never leaving when the last words to a child or my husband were negative or harsh. I made this decision as a newlywed after I heard a pastor share the story of the death of his daughter.

Normally a loving father, one morning he was angry with his daughter for dawdling in heading out the door to school. His words cut and wounded her. His day was long and packed with responsibility, and he didn't arrive home until after her bedtime. She died that night in her sleep from an undiagnosed aneurism. His last words haunted him for years as he struggled to forgive himself. I never want any of my loved ones to struggle that way, so I want to make sure the last words shared are always words of love, even if a conflict cannot be immediately resolved.

In the same way, I learned quickly how the first words I shared with my husband set the tone for our time together that day or evening. For example, I always want to greet him better than our dog might. If the puppy is more excited than I am, there is a problem! I also learned early on that if I chose words that complimented Bill instead of criticized him, even if he came home later than expected, the evening could be saved by a greeting of grace, or ruined by an angry accusation.

Let's take a lesson from some of the first and last words of Paul's letters to the church:

---

* *A man has joy in an apt answer, and how delightful is a timely word!* (Proverbs 15:23, NASB)

Greetings of Goodness.

Grace and peace to you from God our Father and the Lord Jesus Christ. I thank my God every time I remember you. In all my prayers for all of you, I always pray with joy because of your partnership in the gospel from the first day until now, being confident of this, that he who began a good work in you will carry it on to completion until the day of Christ Jesus. It is right for me to feel this way about all of you, since I have you in my heart. (Philippians 1:2-7)

To the holy and faithful . . . Grace and peace to you from God our Father. We always thank God, the Father of our Lord Jesus Christ, when we pray for you, because we have heard of your faith in Christ Jesus and of the love you have for all the saints—the faith and love that spring from the hope that is stored up for you in heaven. (Colossians 1:2-5)

Last Words of Love.

Peace to the brothers, and love with faith from God the Father and the Lord Jesus Christ. Grace to all who love our Lord Jesus Christ with an undying love. (Ephesians 6:23-24)

Finally, brethren, rejoice, be made complete, be comforted, be like-minded, live in peace; and the God of love and peace will be with you. Greet one another with a holy kiss. All the saints greet you. The grace of the Lord Jesus Christ, and the love of God, and the fellowship of the Holy Spirit, be with you all. (2 Corinthians 13:11-14, NASB)

Today, bookend your relationships with first and last words of love.

✳ **Send Up a Message:** Lord, help me greet and depart with love. Amen.

✳ **Text Helps:** Your first and last words might be words of love, words of encouragement, or even words of prayer. These verses give more insight into the words you might share:
EPHESIANS 4:15—[Speak] the truth in love.

COLOSSIANS 4:6—Let your conversation be always full of grace.

HEBREWS 3:13; 10:25—Encourage one another daily, as long as it is called Today, so that none of you may be hardened by sin's deceitfulness. . . . Let us encourage one another—and all the more as you see the Day approaching.

1 TIMOTHY 2:1—I [Paul] urge, then, first of all, that requests, prayers, intercession and thanksgiving be made for everyone.

❋ **Your Turn:** Write or text a message back to God about your life, what you read, or a request on your heart:

_____

_____

_____

_____

_____

_____

LOL

The Last Word

When our [Pam and Bill's] son Caleb was a preschooler, he was incredibly stubborn when it came to bedtime or obedience to our requests. Instead of saying "No!" in rebellion, he tried to delay obedience or prolong bedtime with a series of ridiculous questions that were prefaced with the words "Just one more thing."

One night, in exasperation, my husband said, "Caleb, you cannot delay any longer. You will be punished if you say even one more time, 'Just one more thing.' So Son, get in there, pick up those toys, brush your teeth, and get in bed!"

Caleb replied, "Just one more thing—Dad, what would my punishment be?"

❋ ❋ ❋

Speak the Same Language

Text Message: *Kp wtch ovr t dr of my lps.*

"What shirt are you going to wear, honey?" I [Dawn] asked my husband.

"The blue one," he replied.

Oh, right. Half of my husband's clothes are blue. I describe his shirts as sky blue, robin-egg blue, baby blue, Persian blue, powder blue, periwinkle, sapphire, royal blue, navy, and indigo—but not Bob. They're all just "blue." But what can I expect from a man who sees no logic in owning one style of shoes in four colors and doesn't understand the concept of "fat clothes"?

Most of the struggles that couples experience come when there are communication breakdowns. As Pam and her husband, Bill, illustrate in their book *Men Are Like Waffles, Women Are Like Spaghetti,*[1] men and women don't think alike; so how can we hope to speak in ways that cross that great divide?

How do we speak the same language? We don't! We learn to adjust, pray for wisdom, and try to explain things in terms of the other person's perspective.

These principles of good communication work in *any* relationship:

1. Understand that God *wants* you to communicate well, so you need to practice!
2. Speak with humility, respect, patience, and peace.
3. Allow time to communicate. Slow down and plan for communication.
4. Listen. Concentrate on a person's words without interrupting or thinking about what you want to say instead of listening. Allow for natural breaks in the conversation; don't do all the talking!

---

* *Set a guard, O LORD, over my mouth; keep watch over the door of my lips!* (Psalm 141:3, ESV)

5. Understand that communication involves nonverbal elements too.
6. Speak the truth, but always in love; be careful about timing.
7. Guard your lips. Once you've said it, you can't take it back.

❋ **Send Up a Message:** Lord, teach me how to encourage others, and help me guard my lips from hurtful speech. Amen.

❋ **Text Helps:** The Bible addresses many issues regarding relationship building, especially the topic of communication, as these verses illustrate:

PROVERBS 18:13—He who answers before listening—that is his folly and his shame.

PROVERBS 21:23—He who guards his mouth and his tongue keeps himself from calamity.

PROVERBS 25:11—A word aptly spoken is like apples of gold in settings of silver.

JAMES 1:19—My dear brothers, take note of this: Everyone should be quick to listen, slow to speak and slow to become angry.

❋ **Your Turn:** Write or text a message back to God about your life, what you read, or a request on your heart:

____

____

____

____

____

LOL

And That's When the Fight Started . . .

I asked my wife, "Where do you want to go for our anniversary?" It warmed my heart to see her face melt in sweet appreciation.

"Somewhere I haven't been in a long time!" she said.

So I suggested, "How about the kitchen?" And that's when the fight started.

When I got home last night, my wife demanded that I take her someplace expensive. So, I took her to a gas station. And that's when the fight started.

A woman is standing looking in the bedroom mirror. She isn't happy with what she sees and says to her husband, "I feel horrible; I look old, fat, and ugly. I really need you to pay me a compliment."

The husband replies, "Your eyesight is near perfect." And that's when the fight started.

My wife was hinting about what she wanted for our upcoming anniversary. She said, "I want something shiny that goes from 0 to 150 in about three seconds." I bought her a scale. And that's when the fight started.[2]

---

1. Bill and Pam Farrel, *Men Are Like Waffles, Women Are Like Spaghetti* (Eugene, OR: Harvest House, 2001).

2. Original source unknown. Adapted from "And Then the Fight Started," Bloggits.com, www.bloggits.com/2009/2/4/Jokes/General/And-then-the-fight-started/ (accessed March 15, 2010).

Rearranging Deck Chairs

Peter Walsh, the professional organizer on the hit show *Clean Sweep*, once expressed exactly how I [Dawn] felt one day as I tried to find space in my house. Walsh wrote, "Rearrange the deck chairs on the *Titanic* as much as you want, the ship is still going down!"[1] In my overstuffed home, I suddenly realized that all my "prized possessions" owned *me*. I whined to God, "How did I get here, Lord? How did I accumulate all this stuff?" I thought I heard the Spirit say, "Well, duh . . . you bought it all!"

The real cost of keeping my clutter went beyond the value of each item. Clutter took over my home, robbing me of much-needed breathing space and affecting my family relationships. It wasn't a matter of rearranging deck chairs anymore. The stuff just had to go. It wasn't easy, but I needed to reevaluate what was most important to me and let the clutter go.

Walsh encourages his clients to imagine the lives they want to achieve—their ideal home. Once they have a clear understanding of this, the home purging flows from that vision. It's easier to eliminate things that don't belong. "It's you or your stuff," Walsh says. "Make the choice."[2]

Marcia Ramsland, author of *Simplify Your Space: Create Order and Reduce Stress*, agrees: "Remember, one pile sitting out is the beginning of a complicated life. Keep your life simple and put the pile away. Do that by putting each item in a drawer or cabinet where it belongs and keep it in that one place. Soon your 'homeless' clutter items will find a home, and you'll relax looking at clean countertops across your home and office."[3] This is good advice for all of us. Letting go can be difficult, but if the item has no need and no home, release it.

What's true in our homes is crucial in our hearts. Once we get a clear

---

* *Let us throw off everything that hinders and the sin that so easily entangles.* (Hebrews 12:1)

understanding of who we are in Christ and what the Father has called us to do, it's *much* easier to pare down our possessions and eliminate whatever robs us of effective ministry or drains away our time. Because we desire God's will (His plans and agenda for our lives), junk in our hearts has to go. We must lay aside all the "weight" (hindrances and sins) that clutters our lives, and when we do, we'll experience new freedom and peace. We won't have to repeatedly rearrange distracting "deck chairs" because we'll have found true rest in the hammock of God's will.

Is anything cluttering your heart or distracting you from God's plans for your home, work, life, or ministry? What needs to go so that God can powerfully use you in the days to come? Don't just shuffle things around. Clean house!

✳ **Send Up a Message:** Father, give me fresh vision for my home and life, and help me eliminate the "junk" in my heart. Amen.

✳ **Text Helps:** After you read the following verses, ask the Holy Spirit to roam around the rooms of your heart and point out anything that doesn't belong in your life. Don't rush Him. Listen carefully. If you're willing, say, "Yes, Lord," and then obey. You'll be so glad you did!

PSALM 139:23-24—Search me, O God, and know my heart; test me and know my anxious thoughts. See if there is any offensive way in me, and lead me in the way everlasting.

MATTHEW 6:21—Where your treasure is, there your heart will be also.

1 CORINTHIANS 6:11—You were washed, you were sanctified, you were justified in the name of the Lord Jesus Christ and by the Spirit of our God.

EPHESIANS 4:29-31—Do not let any unwholesome talk come out of your mouths, but only what is helpful for building others up according to their needs, that it may benefit those who listen. And do not grieve the Holy Spirit of God, with whom you were sealed for the day of redemption. Get rid of all bitterness, rage and anger, brawling and slander, along with every form of malice.

✳ **Your Turn:** Write or text a message back to God about your life, what you read, or a request on your heart:

_____

_____

_____

_____

_____

_____

LOL

Say What?

One day a housework-challenged husband decided to wash his sweatshirt.

Seconds after he stepped into the laundry room, he shouted to his wife, "What setting do I use on the washing machine?"

"It depends," she replied. "What does it say on your shirt?"

He yelled back, "Denver Broncos!"[4]

And for those moms with housework-challenged kids . . .

Our friend shares this story about the logic of when to clean house:

I was gone all weekend at a soccer tournament with my daughter, Annie. When I returned, I found my twin boys' books were off the shelf. Their mattresses, blankets, and pillows were off the bed and heaped at the bottom of the stairs—a landing ramp for their jumping contest. Wadded newspapers and school papers were strewn about like fall leaves. Dirty clothes were lying willy-nilly where the boys had discarded them.

To be honest, I wasn't really surprised that my husband wasn't a better house manager while I was gone, but the thought of putting the house to rights seemed overwhelming, especially with having to be at work next morning.

Then one of the twins, Lewis, came to drag me upstairs so that I could kiss him good night. "Where were you?" he asked after snuggling up in his covers.

I explained about the soccer tournament. He asked, "When are you going to teach Sissy to drive?"

"When are you going to learn to put away your books?" I responded.

"Oh, that!" he said. "I was going to, then I remembered it's more fun when you help. I *waited* for you." He said this as if cleaning up the books with me was as special as opening Christmas presents.[5]

1. Peter Walsh, *It's All Too Much: An Easy Plan for Living a Richer Life with Less Stuff* (New York: Free Press, 2007), 10.
2. Ibid, 14.
3. Marcia Ramsland, correspondence with authors, July, 5 2009. Used by permission.
4. Original source unknown. Quoted in Mary Marlow Leverette, "Clean Jokes from the Laundry Room," adapted from About.com, http://laundry.about.com/od/laundrybasics/a/laundryhumor.htm (accessed March 15, 2010).
5. Personal story shared with authors. Used by permission.

Worrywart

Text Message: *U wl kp hm n prfct pce whos mnd s styd on U.*

My [Dawn's] dad was a worrier. His childhood nickname was "Wartie," because he was such a "worrywart." Long before I understood this term, I thought worrywarts came from touching ugly frogs! Like Dad, I tend to worry about things that will probably never happen. Worry can be a mild or serious disorder. On any level, the relentless, nagging thought that something will go wrong robs us of something our loving God wants us to enjoy—His peace. True peace comes when we submit to God's care and authority.

Much has been written about the tragic story behind the great hymn "It Is Well with My Soul," but few know that the familiar first line— "When peace like a river attendeth my way"[1]—was drawn from Isaiah 48:18. "If only you had paid attention to my commands," Isaiah wrote, speaking for God, "your peace would have been like a river, your righteousness like the waves of the sea." Like the author of the song who lost his family at sea and then wrote about how God gave him supernatural peace to face such loss, we, too, gain peace in the same way—when we give in to God's plan, even when we don't understand all the details of that plan.

We may be tempted to worry, but God will guard our hearts with His peace when our minds are "stayed" or focused on Him. His peace will flood over us, refresh our souls, and help us move forward with confidence.

You will keep him in perfect peace, whose mind is stayed on You, because he trusts in You. (Isaiah 26:3, NKJV)

Pam and I serve in an organization, Seasoned Sisters, which seeks to encourage women. When things get tough for a sister, we give each other frogs: frog magnets, frog socks, frog cards, and other frog paraphernalia. We smile when we think of frogs, because F-R-O-G stands for "Fully Rely On God"—a perfect prescription for worry. If you want peace, FROG it.

✽ **Send Up a Message:** Lord, I don't want worry to rob me of Your peace. I choose to rely on Your care. Amen.

✽ **Text Helps:** When do you feel most anxious? Read the remedy for an anxious heart, and then apply God's prescription!

LUKE 12:25-26—Who of you by worrying can add a single hour to his life? Since you cannot do this very little thing, why do you worry about the rest?

JOHN 14:27—[Jesus said,] "Peace I leave with you; my peace I give you. I do not give to you as the world gives. Do not let your hearts be troubled and do not be afraid."

PHILIPPIANS 4:6-7—Do not be anxious about anything, but in everything, by prayer and petition, with thanksgiving, present your requests to God. And the peace of God, which transcends all understanding, will guard your hearts and your minds in Christ Jesus.

✽ **Your Turn:** Write or text a message back to God about your life, what you read, or a request on your heart:

_____

_____

_____

_____

_____

_____

_____

LOL

Speaking of Frogs . . .

A guy is taking a walk and sees a frog on the side of the road. As he comes closer, the frog starts to talk: "Kiss me and I will turn into a princess."

The guy picks the frog up and puts it in his pocket. The frog starts shouting, "Hey! Didn't you hear me? I'm a princess. Just kiss me and I will be yours."

The guy takes the frog out of his pocket and smiles at it and [then] puts it back. The frog is really frustrated. "I don't get it. Why won't you kiss me? I will turn into a beautiful princess and do anything you ask."

The guy says, "Look, I'm a computer geek. I don't have time for women. But a talking frog is very cool!"[2]

1. Horatio G. Spafford, "It Is Well with My Soul," 1873, www.cyberhymnal.org/htm/i/t/i/
    itiswell.htm. Public domain.
2. Original source unknown. Quoted in Jonathan Danylko, "Humor: A Frog Princess and
    a Programmer," DCS Media, March 23, 2006, www.dcs-media.com/webworthy/
    humor/humor-a-frog-princess-and-a-programmer.aspx (accessed March 15, 2010).

Out of Hiding

Text Message: *4 a mns wys r n ful vew of t LORD.** *

We all have secrets. We may hide who we are and what we do from others, but we can never hide from God. I [Dawn] remember the day I told God, "I'm not keeping any more secrets from You, Lord." Like that was a news flash to God! That sounds silly, of course, since He knows everything about me. But what I meant in my heart was, "I'm going to admit who I am and what's going on in my life."

I used to view God as this super-mean Judge in the sky, always waiting for me to mess up. I imagined Him pointing an "Aha!" finger my way. That was such a pitiful view of the One who loves me so much (John 3:16).

God is *grieved* by my sins, and He wants me to bring them out in the open before Him—no more secrets—so I can live in the joy-filled freedom of forgiveness.

We have all fallen short of God's holy standards (Romans 3:23), but seeing our sin is tricky sometimes, because sin deceives us, and our enemy, Satan, wants to trip us up with lies.

For a time I [Pam] worked in the school system with blind students. My supervisors were thrilled to hear that Bill and I were moving to attend seminary and graduate school, and they encouraged me to keep working with the disabled. One teacher gave me a braille typewriter—with one little condition. "Just take it," she said, "but don't let anyone see you take it. We have so many, and no one will need this. It can help you get a job."

I was initially excited because I knew I'd need a good paying job to help put my husband through seminary. I packed it away in our boxes, but then God's Spirit began whispering to my heart: "Pam, was that hers

---

* *A man's ways are in full view of the* LORD, *and he examines all his paths.* (Proverbs 5:21)

to give away? Doesn't it belong to the students and the school district? Pam, could it possibly be right to put your pastor-husband through grad school with an instrument you had to sneak off campus? Where's the integrity in that?"

I knew it just wasn't worth it to cut corners. I decided to walk the machine right back into its home classroom. At once, peace came to my heart, sleep came easy that night, and in the end, after we moved, I worked for Insight for Living, the radio ministry of Dr. Charles Swindoll. I believe that because I was faithful to not keep secrets in the little things, I gained the opportunity to work for one of the godliest leaders of our time.

God wants us to stop rationalizing and blaming others and just come clean with Him. He will bring every hidden thing to light (1 Corinthians 4:5), so trying to hide sin is foolish. God loves us too much to allow us to continue in our sins, whether they are hidden or willful (Psalm 19:12-13). True freedom comes when we lay the hidden recesses of our hearts open before the light of Scripture.

So come out of hiding and into God's light.

❋ **Send Up a Message:** Father God, I am so grateful for Your forgiveness, because of what Jesus has done for me on the cross. Help me live every day in transparency and honesty before You. Amen!

❋ **Text Helps:** It's not always comfortable to examine our lives for sin, but it's a good exercise when we think of the end result—coming clean with God and connecting with Him. As you read the following scriptures, let God search your heart.

PSALM 66:18—If I had cherished sin in my heart, the Lord would not have listened.

ECCLESIASTES 12:14—God will bring every deed into judgment, including every hidden thing, whether it is good or evil.

1 JOHN 1:8-9—If we claim to be without sin, we deceive ourselves and the truth is not in us. If we confess our sins, he is faithful and just and will forgive us our sins and purify us from all unrighteousness.

❈ **Your Turn:** Write or text a message back to God about your life, what you read, or a request on your heart:

_____

_____

_____

_____

_____

_____

LOL

Secret Sins

Three pastors went to a religious convention and decided to share a hotel room. As the night wore on, the first pastor said, "I know. Let's confess our secret sins one to another. I'll start. My secret sin is that I just love to gamble. When I go out of town, it's 'cha-ching, cha-ching, let the machines ring!'"

The second pastor said, "My secret sin is that I just hate working. I copy all my sermons from those given by other pastors."

The third pastor grinned and said, "Ah, dear friends. My secret sin is gossiping, and I can't wait to get out of this room!"[1]

---

1. Original source unknown. Adapted from "Secret Sin," Christian-Jokes.org, www. christian-jokes.org/jokes29.html (accessed March 15, 2010).

Normal Choices

**Text Message: *Wlk by t Spirit,
& u wl nt grtfy t dsrs o t flsh*** *

I [Dawn] can choose what I eat. Knowing that truth is good, but acting wisely on it is crucial to my health. In my flesh, I tend to compromise with nutrition choices. I once went through the grocery checkout with a stockpile of nutritious, low-fat, low-calorie foods . . . and three half gallons of on-sale ice cream!

As the clerk scanned my items, she looked up at me and grinned when the ice cream approached. "For the *kids*, right?" she said. I turned red. The clerk noticed my inconsistency. The ice cream was my reward for "being good" even though it sabotaged my healthy choices. Who was I fooling?

We truly reap what we sow in our choices. There are consequences for every decision we make, good or bad. Most of us don't want to deal with poor nutrition choices until we hear, "Doctor's orders!" In Genesis 1, God created all things and declared them "good," so we have an incredible smorgasbord of healthy food choices; but God also expects us to be smart and practice discipline, not gluttony. We must keep our bodies, the dwelling place of God's Spirit, "blameless" until Christ's return (1 Thessalonians 5:23).

So it is with all of our choices. To choose according to the compulsions of our flesh is "normal," and it might very well be what the majority of the population does. But God expects us to make wise, godly choices, whether they're about food, finances, habits, relationships, moral conduct, business ethics, or any other aspect of our lives. I'm not saying this is easy, and believe me, it's a struggle for me, too.

---

* *Walk by the Spirit, and you will not gratify the desires of the flesh.* (Galatians 5:16, ESV)

Instead of going with the status quo and doing what you normally would do, before you make a choice today, simply pray and ask God, "Is this wise? Is this healthy? Is this best?" As you spend time with God, whether in His Word or in devotionals like this one, what is good, normal, and healthy will become easier to spot. Taking a split second to pray about a choice will also be a safeguard for your life and future.

❊ **Send Up a Message:** Father, teach me how to make wise choices. I want to obey Your Spirit and Word. Amen.

❊ **Text Helps:** The Bible is full of wise counsel to help us overcome our weaknesses, bad habits, and addictions, but we must act on this truth with faith in God and His power. These encouraging words can help:

ROMANS 12:2—Do not conform any longer to the pattern of this world, but be transformed by the renewing of your mind. Then you will be able to test and approve what God's will is—his good, pleasing and perfect will.

GALATIANS 6:7-8—Do not be deceived: God cannot be mocked. A man reaps what he sows. The one who sows to please his sinful nature, from that nature will reap destruction; the one who sows to please the Spirit, from the Spirit will reap eternal life.

1 PETER 5:8—Be self-controlled and alert. Your enemy the devil prowls around like a roaring lion looking for someone to devour.

1 JOHN 5:4—Everyone born of God overcomes the world. This is the victory that has overcome the world, even our faith.

❊ **Your Turn:** Write or text a message back to God about your life, what you read, or a request on your heart:

_____

_____

_____

_____

_____

_____

LOL

Laughter That Burns!

I [Pam] am a member of a wonderful First Place 4 Health small group that promotes and encourages healthy lifestyle choices. We all try to help each other make wise food choices, and most of us are also over 40. One day we were commiserating online about fast foods, and one of my friends got us the calorie count of a popular Dairy Queen frozen dessert called a Blizzard.

She and her assistant were in the office looking up calorie counts for the different flavored Blizzards and wondered why the Health Blizzard would have more calories than a strawberry one, especially since it claimed to be a *Health* Blizzard. When her assistant brought in the Blizzard printout, the woman noticed she wasn't wearing her glasses. Looking at the list, the woman said, "This isn't a *Health* Blizzard; it's a *Heath* blizzard!"[1]

Yep, that one *L* and the fact it was a candy-bar Blizzard might have added a few calories, but for all of us in the group with bifocals, it also provided a much-needed laugh. According to a study published in the *International Journal of Obesity,* "Laughter really is the best medicine for a weight problem. . . . *Just 15 minutes of laughter a day will burn 10 to 40 calories,* depending on a person's weight and the intensity of the laughter. That's enough to shift between 1 and 4 [pounds] a year" (emphasis added).[2]

So, skip the Blizzard and laugh out loud with a friend instead.

1. Carole Lewis, e-mail message to Pam, March 18, 2009. Used by permission.
2. M. S. Buchowski et al., "Energy Expenditure of Genuine Laughter," *International Journal of Obesity* 31 (January 2007): 131–37, http://faculty.chass.ncsu.edu/porter/documents/Buckowskienergyexpend.pdf, cited in Juliette Kellow, "Laugh Yourself Slim," Weight Loss Resources, www.weightlossresources.co.uk/calories/burning_calories/laughing-burns-calories.htm (accessed March 11, 2010).

Learn from Your Critics

Text Message: *no lngr crtisz 1 nthr.***

Critics are everywhere. Criticism can hurt us as surely as a knife in the back; it tears down and destroys. Even "constructive" criticism can be hurtful when it's unkind or unnecessary. I [Dawn] remember a woman who praised my sewing. "Oh, how lovely," she said. "You did a good job, but . . ." Then she listed every flaw she saw, and her praise faded away.

I've felt the knife of criticism many times. Remembering that pain, I'm careful not to wield the nasty weapon myself. I've forgiven those who cut me, giving them the benefit of the doubt when I can and handing them over to God when I'm sure they meant me harm. To do so requires humility and trust in God's control. Only He knows whether they are striking out because of insecurity or their own miserable pain. Perhaps they don't even know how their critical words sound—how they slice and injure others. When appropriate, I've learned to thank my critics for their advice. I certainly need to grow, and I'm well aware of my flaws.

I [Pam] have learned that same truth, so when a woman came up to me after I had spoken and said, "Pam, I love you. You are so real; you even have this little pooch!" as she patted my tummy roll, I just laughed and said, "Bless your heart!" I knew she meant her words as a compliment, so I chose not to be offended.

God observes our responses as well as our critics' barbs. He also notices when we are the critic. My [Pam's] son decided not to pursue a friendship because the person was so critical of everyone in sight. The food was never hot enough, or the service was never fast enough or personal enough. My son found himself always covering for or apologizing for the behavior of his friend. He, of course, was brave enough to point it out to his friend—

---

* *Let us no longer criticize one another.* (Romans 14:13, HCSB)

yep, you guessed it; he was criticized for pointing it out! However, that same son learned from this experience, and he is now one of the most encouraging, gracious men I know. He is always affirming, even to strangers, waitstaff, maids, door attendants—he thanks everyone for everything!

It's a rare day when we turn a critic into a supporter or a close friend, but love can work miracles. Love can also help us be a miracle giver, because our words can make someone else's day! Just as a gentle answer turns away wrath (Proverbs 15:1), a humble response can disarm antagonism—or thoughtlessness.

❋ **Send Up a Message:** Nudge me, Lord, when I have a proud, critical spirit; and help me learn from my critics. Amen.

❋ **Text Helps:** We need to listen to our critics' words, and then go before the Lord to ask Him if the words are true. We also need to be careful not to judge others. These two principles are spelled out in the following verses:

MATTHEW 7:1-2—Do not judge, or you too will be judged. For in the same way you judge others, you will be judged, and with the measure you use, it will be measured to you.

ROMANS 14:10-13—You, then, why do you judge your brother? Or why do you look down on your brother? For we will all stand before God's judgment seat. It is written: "As surely as I live," says the Lord, "every knee will bow before me; every tongue will confess to God." So then, each of us will give an account of himself to God. Therefore let us stop passing judgment on one another. Instead, make up your mind not to put any stumbling block or obstacle in your brother's way.

❋ **Your Turn:** Write or text a message back to God about your life, what you read, or a request on your heart:

_____

_____

_____

_____

LOL

The Other Hut

A man was stranded on a proverbial deserted Pacific island for years.

Finally one day, a boat came sailing into view, and the man frantically waved to draw the skipper's attention. The boat came near the island, and the sailor got out and greeted the stranded man.

After a while the sailor asked, "What are those three huts you have here?"

"Well, that's my house there."

"What's that next hut?" asked the sailor.

"I built that hut to be my church."

"What about the other hut?"

"Oh, that's where I used to go to church."[1]

---

1. Adapted from "Church Hopping," Basic Jokes, http://www.basicjokes.com/djoke. php?id=163 (accessed March 13, 2010).

Eager Sponges

Text Message: *Trn up a chld n t wy he shld go.* *

Children are all eyes and ears. They observe parents and imitate what is modeled, even if the parents are unaware of the lessons they're teaching. When parents least expect it, children take note and internalize what they see. Parents are children's first teachers, but not always their best teachers.

A teacher in a parenting session told his audience members to point to their noses. The only problem was, the teacher pointed to his chin. The audience also pointed to their chins. This is the challenge in parenting. What we *do* is indeed more powerful than what we *say*, and this is especially true with small children. They might hear what we say, but they will mirror our actions, so we must be careful that our actions line up with God's truth and our most treasured beliefs and values.

The Bible says we are to teach our families God's Word wherever we are and at all times of the day. In *The Message*, Deuteronomy 6:6-7 includes a powerful admonition (verse 7): "Get them [God's laws] inside of you and then get them inside your children." It is said that a child's values are better caught than taught.

Dr. Edward Hindson, Assistant Chancellor at Liberty University, says there are three essential elements in the parent-child relationship—instruction (what you say), influence (what you do), and image (what you are). "Many parents mistakenly assume that child discipline is simply instructing children by telling them what to do," Hindson said, "[but] . . . instruction is only part of the process. Your actions may have contradicted your instruction."[1]

---

* *Train up a child in the way he should go [and in keeping with his individual gift or bent], and when he is old he will not depart from it.* (Proverbs 22:6, AMP)

Children are eager sponges, absorbing the truths that we most cherish, as evidenced by our actions if not our words. We must be careful that our children soak up the right things!

✸ **Send Up a Message:** People are watching me, Lord. I want to be an authentic Christian. Amen.

✸ **Text Helps:** Consider the following scriptures about the role of parents in modeling spiritual truths. What does the Bible say is the role of parents in helping their children understand the ways and will of God?

DEUTERONOMY 6:4-9—Hear, O Israel: The LORD our God, the LORD is one. Love the LORD your God with all your heart and with all your soul and with all your strength. These commandments that I give you today are to be upon your hearts. Impress them on your children. Talk about them when you sit at home and when you walk along the road, when you lie down and when you get up. Tie them as symbols on your hands and bind them on your foreheads. Write them on the doorframes of your houses and on your gates.

EPHESIANS 6:4—Fathers, do not exasperate your children; instead, bring them up in the training and instruction of the Lord.

✸ **Your Turn:** Write or text a message back to God about your life, what you read, or a request on your heart:

_____

_____

_____

_____

_____

_____

_____

_____

LOL

Almost Right

The faith of a child can be inspiring—but children sometimes aren't completely accurate in their comprehension of the Bible's principles. One of our friends, Holly, shared an example with us from her daughter's life. Her daughter was learning about the concept of being a "fisher of men" in her Sunday school class. (A *fisher of men* is someone who brings people to Jesus.) She came home so excited, wanting to share her news.

"Mommy, teacher told us that we should not fish for fish; we should fish for men!" the girl gushed.

When Holly asked her, "What are we supposed to do once we catch the men?" her daughter proudly announced, "We eat them!"

Another time, Holly wanted to talk to her little girl about becoming a Christian. So she casually mentioned, "You know, there's only one way to get to heaven . . ."

To that, her daughter quickly replied, "Yeah, you have to die!"[2]

1. Dr. Edward E. Hindson, *The Total Family* (Wheaton, IL: Tyndale, 1980), 72.
2. Holly Hanson, personal stories shared with authors. Used by permission.

Perpetual Heritage

Text Message: *U hv gvn me t hritg.* *

Alline Lihme frames her family's handwritten recipes for her kitchen wall. A lovely, decorative touch, the recipes also provide an instant link to Alline's past, and she has shared some with her children for their walls. "It's an easy way to teach children about generations who have been gathered to their fathers," Alline said.[1]

I [Dawn] love the idea so much that I may frame my Grandma Dorothy's Potato Soup with Egg Rivels recipe. When my sons married, I gave both of their wives the Wilson family cookbook, crammed with recipes my sons and other family members enjoy.

Passing on recipes is more than the recipes themselves; it represents and preserves the traditions of earlier generations. Grandma's potato-soup recipe isn't about the humble spud. It's about the memories we shared while peeling potatoes, and the love we shared around her table.

More than recipes, I want my sons to know that both of my grandmothers and grandfathers testified to their faith in Jesus Christ. We knew they loved the Lord. I want my boys to know that their dad and I love the Lord too.

Like Eunice and Lois in Bible times (2 Timothy 1:5; 3:15), I desire for my family to enjoy a *perpetual* godly heritage. I'm praying that my sons will grow in their relationships with God and pass on a clear understanding of who He is to my granddaughters. Time passes quickly. Worthy values—integrity in Christ, a Christian worldview, and an eternal perspective—must be our priority in any generation.

---

* *You have given me the heritage of those who fear, revere, and honor Your name.* (Psalm 61:5, AMP)

Think about your own family. What meaningful traditions have been passed down to you? Maybe a recipe? A family ritual? A rite of passage or a special ceremony? Name at least two of your family traditions:

1. _____

2. _____

Now, what traditions are you passing down to your children? What meaningful moments do you want your children to remember? Pray and ask God to show you some ways to pass on your values and beliefs from generation to generation.

❋ **Send Up a Message:** Father, show me how I can share Your love and truth with this generation. Amen.

❋ **Text Helps:** In many of the Old Testament accounts of the leaders of Israel, we can read about the heritage of these kings. Some parents and grandparents were godly; some were not. As you read the following scriptures, think about the influence you have on today's generation.

EPHESIANS 6:1-4—Children, obey your parents in the Lord, for this is right. "Honor your father and mother"—which is the first commandment with a promise—"that it may go well with you and that you may enjoy long life on the earth." Fathers, do not exasperate your children; instead, bring them up in the training and instruction of the Lord.

2 TIMOTHY 1:5; 3:15-17—I have been reminded of your sincere faith, which first lived in your grandmother Lois and in your mother Eunice and, I am persuaded, now lives in you also. . . . From infancy you have known the holy Scriptures, which are able to make you wise for salvation through faith in Christ Jesus. All Scripture is God-breathed and is useful for teaching, rebuking, correcting and training in righteousness, so that the man of God may be thoroughly equipped for every good work.

✳ **Your Turn:** Write or text a message back to God about your life, what you read, or a request on your heart:

_____

_____

_____

_____

LOL

Sharing Grandparents

Author Nancy Sebastian Meyer shares a story from those "Bring Your Parent to School" days:

Our daughter's first-grade teacher invited the children's grandparents to a special celebration in the classroom. Becky was blessed to have four grandparents living at that time and able to attend. As the party got started, the teacher asked Becky if she would be willing to share one of her sets of grandparents with a child who didn't have any special guests.

Becky matter-of-factly responded to the little girl in need, "Would you like ones with or without oxygen?" motioning to her paternal grandfather who had just started toting around an oxygen canister and then to my dad. All of the adults burst out laughing—and I think Papa laughed the hardest![2]

---

1. Alline Lihme, personal story shared with authors. Used by permission.
2. Nancy Sebastian Meyer, personal story shared with authors. Used by permission.

God's Loving Presence

Text Message: *Thr is no fr n lv. Bt prfct lv drvs out fr.* *

What would you do if you got a text message reading, "Nd pryrs! Serious issues hv cm up. Cnt shr details yt"? I [Dawn] received this message one day from my husband, who was on the other side of the world in a pre-dominantly Muslim country. Bob was asking me to pray immediately—but for what? Was there a problem concerning his ministry? Or worse, was he in danger? When I needed courage most, fear flooded my heart.

Instead of wallowing in that fear and mental torment, I turned to the Lord and found peace as I rested in His presence. *Lord,* I prayed, *I have no idea what is going on, but You do. I ask You to give my husband safety, wisdom, peace, and whatever else he needs in this moment.*

Later, Bob shared that the Lord brought exactly the right people into his path to keep him safe, and a complete reversal in leaders' attitudes that allowed for effective ministry.

Knowing that God is in control on the other side of the world as surely as in my living room was a comfort that day. God knows about our anxious thoughts, and He cares. The incredible truth is that God knows our needs before we even ask, and He may already have an answer on the way. We may only hear silence, but God hasn't left His throne—He is still in control—and He is always with us. The silence is not empty but full with His presence. In the quiet, we must wait for Him with courage.

What are your concerns and fears today? Are you concerned about someone in your family? Are you fearful about the future? Are you bur-dened and anxious, or overwhelmed by the chaos in your world? Just as Jesus could sleep through a violent storm (Mark 4:35-41), you can be calm

---

* *There is no fear in love. But perfect love drives out fear.* (1 John 4:18)

instead of panicky when you're grounded in God's love. Take a moment and think of what's concerning you right now.

Remind yourself that "Yr gr8 God wll mv u 4wrd 2 peace."

❋ **Send Up a Message:** Lord, I thank You today for Your love and sovereign control. Amen.

❋ **Text Helps:** Read Mark 4:35-41 to get a glimpse of how Jesus, our Example, practiced resting in His Father's presence. Then select one of the following verses to remind you that God's loving presence is powerful, and you can always reach out to Him in prayer.

PSALM 27:14—Wait for the LORD; be strong and take heart and wait for the LORD.

PSALM 103:11—As high as the heavens are above the earth, so great is his love for those who fear him.

ISAIAH 65:24—Before they call I [the Lord] will answer; while they are still speaking I will hear.

MATTHEW 6:8—Your Father knows what you need before you ask him.

❋ **Your Turn:** Write or text a message back to God about your life, what you read, or a request on your heart:

_____

_____

_____

_____

LOL

Are You There?

While vacationing with my family, we were traveling down the highway and we all needed to use the restroom. I [Pam] stopped at a rest area and headed to the restroom while Bill and the guys headed to theirs. I was barely sitting down when I heard a voice from the other stall saying, "Hi, how are you?"

I'm friendly, but I do think there are certain times that conversation is not needed—and this was one of them! But not wanting to be rude, I answered, "Doing just fine, I guess."

And the other person said, "So what are you up to?"

Okay, this is weird! I thought. *What kind of question is that?* I was thinking this was too bizarre, so I said, "Uhhh, I'm like you—just traveling!"

At this point, just trying to get out as fast as I could, I heard another question.

"Can I come over?"

Ok, that question was just too uncomfortable for me, but I figured I could just be polite and end the conversation. I said, "No, I don't think so. I'm a little BUSY right now!"

Then I heard the woman say nervously, "Listen, I'll have to call you back. There's some crazy woman in the other stall who keeps answering all my questions!"

(To avoid embarrassment, I stayed in my stall a really long time waiting for her to leave and exit the rest stop. When I finally exited the restroom, my men looked at me and asked, "What took you so long?")

Cell phones!

Daily Bread

Text Message: *Gv us ths day r dly brd.* *

My [Pam's] friend Margaret served as a missionary in one of the world's poorest countries, Haiti. One day, while leading a Bible study, Margaret was perplexed about how to handle Philippians 4:19: "My God will meet all your needs according to his glorious riches in Christ Jesus."

Margaret writes, "How could I explain this verse about God supplying needs when I wasn't hungry, and my family had a roof over our heads and food on the table? I realized the best method would be to ask my Haitian friends what the verse said to them. Louise, a house servant, replied, 'I would love to put all my children in school, but I can't. I would love for each of them to have a grass mat to sleep on, but they don't. I would love to be able to feed a meal to my family each day, but I can't. But that is okay—God says if I really needed these things, I would have them because He said so.'"

Margaret began to pray that God would indeed move on behalf of her Haitian sisters. Bailing out the whole island, or even those closest to her, was not an option on her own meager missionary budget. God would indeed need to be the Provider. She would do her part, but God would have to do His part.

One day at a prayer meeting, she overheard the prayer of a Haitian neighbor, "Lord, we have been asked to pray about the embargo. I have prayed this for a long time now, and I have nothing else to say. Lord, we have been asked to pray for our daily bread, and I have not had any in four days. Lord, please don't make me bitter."

Margaret's heart broke. After the prayer meeting, Margaret told her Haitian friend, "I can do nothing about the embargo or the government.

---

* *Give us this day our daily bread.* (Matthew 6:11, NKJV)

However, I can do something about the daily bread." Margaret invited the woman to her home later that day. "When my new friend arrived at the house," Margaret said, "I gave her four loaves of bread, some peanut butter, and a gallon of filtered water. She was so grateful for God's bountiful supply.

"The next day I saw her at the mission station and asked her how the bread was. She said it was all gone. Surprised that she didn't make it stretch, I asked why it had been eaten up so quickly. The woman told me that she had shared her 'bounty' with her neighbors. Forty people had had a share of her answer to prayer."

Shortly after this, Margaret received a package from supporters stateside. Because it was a surprise personal gift from the states, sent months before, it was miraculously allowed through the embargo. Its contents included a barrel of flour! That day, a bread-loaf ministry was born. God had provided.[1]

Think about your "needs" list. Are those things really needs, or are they just wants or desires? Sometimes we can lose perspective about how blessed we really are. We can begin to think we deserve better, become discontented, and complain. But as Margaret realized, we should remember that many people around the world truly have to trust God for their daily bread. Consider the needs of those around you. Do you have any "plenty" you can share? In sharing, you'll feel rich.

❋ **Send Up a Message:** Lord, help me be grateful for Your every provision and give me a generous heart so I will be rich in spirit and rich with friendships. Amen.

❋ **Text Helps:** We tend to think that sharing with others means writing a check, but we have many riches to share. Look around your house, in your cupboards, and in your garage. Ask God to open your heart and eyes as you read these scriptures:

PSALM 111:5—He [God] provides food for those who fear him; he remembers his covenant forever.

ROMANS 12:13—Share with God's people who are in need. Practice hospitality.

2 Corinthians 9:8—God is able to make all grace abound to you, so that in all things at all times, having all that you need, you will abound in every good work.

Philippians 4:19—My God will meet all your needs according to his glorious riches in Christ Jesus.

❊ **Your Turn:** Write or text a message back to God about your life, what you read, or a request on your heart:

_____

_____

_____

_____

LOL

In My Heart

A four-year-old girl was at the pediatrician's office for a check-up. As the doctor looked into her ears with an otoscope, he asked, "Do you think I'll find Big Bird in here?"

The little girl stayed silent.

Next, the doctor took a tongue depressor and looked down her throat. He asked, "Do you think I'll find the Cookie Monster down there?"

Again, the little girl was silent.

Then the doctor put a stethoscope to her chest. As he listened to her heart beat, he asked, "Do you think I'll hear Barney in here?"

"Oh, no!" the little girl replied. "Jesus is in my heart. Barney's on my underpants."[2]

---

1. Story used by permission.
2. Original source unknown. Quoted in "Barney," *A Third Serving of Chicken Soup for the Soul,* www.bookpage.com/9606bp/chickensoupforthesoul/chickensoupstories.html (accessed March 15, 2010).

Calm Me Down, Lord!

Text Message: U clmd me dn & chrd me up.*

My [Dawn's] calendar had no more room for events, responsibilities, and meetings, and yet I found myself packing my schedule tighter. It was insanity, and soon I was "beside myself." The earliest documented meaning for this phrase is "out of one's mind."[1]

With my stuffed calendar, I was terribly agitated. My emotions fractured with all the time challenges, and I became frantic and anxious. I knew I was living beyond God's will for my life, and it was time to make some serious changes. God gave me the wisdom to examine my priorities in the light of His Word (Proverbs 31:10-31)—God first, then family, and then ministry and work—and align my schedule according to those priorities.

Some activities simply had to go! I asked God to forgive my foolishness and help me make wiser choices in the future. He calmed me down again, and as I pursued His priorities, He brought fresh strength and passion. Joy and peace replaced anxiety and made me feel less fractured.

I [Pam] can also get overwhelmed with responsibilities, and when I need to carve things out I ask myself these questions:
- Can someone else handle this responsibility?
- Can this task wait for another season when another responsibility is cleared?
- What is the worst thing that might happen if this goes undone?
- Can I delegate this responsibility to a child, another family member or friend, or a volunteer in my circle of influence?

---

* *When I was upset and beside myself, you calmed me down and cheered me up.* (Psalm 94:19, MSG)

- Do I need to review my priorities and rework my schedule so that it reflects biblical priorities—God, marriage, family, work, ministry, etc.?

Are you "beside yourself" today? There's a better alternative. God loves you, and He is eager for you to snuggle beside Him in prayer and embrace His priorities for your life. Take some time to look at your schedule. Is there something that needs to change? If so, start today!

❋ **Send Up a Message:** How I thank You for calming my anxieties, Lord. I rest in Your will today. Amen.

❋ **Text Helps:** As you read about the Proverbs 31 woman, examine your priorities to see how they line up with Scripture. Sometimes, setting those priorities right is a way to rediscover God's peace.

PROVERBS 31:10-13, 15-18, 20-22, 24-31—A wife of noble character who can find? She is worth far more than rubies. Her husband has full confidence in her and lacks nothing of value. She brings him good, not harm, all the days of her life . . . and works with eager hands. . . . She gets up while it is still dark; she provides food for her family and portions for her servant girls. She considers a field and buys it; out of her earnings she plants a vineyard. She sets about her work vigorously; her arms are strong for her tasks. She sees that her trading is profitable, and her lamp does not go out at night. . . . She opens her arms to the poor and extends her hands to the needy. When it snows, she has no fear for her household; for all of them are clothed in scarlet. She makes coverings for her bed; . . . She makes linen garments and sells them, and supplies the merchants with sashes. She is clothed with strength and dignity; she can laugh at the days to come. She speaks with wisdom, and faithful instruction is on her tongue. She watches over the affairs of her household and does not eat the bread of idleness. Her children arise and call her blessed; her husband also, and he praises her: "Many women do noble things, but you surpass them all." Charm is deceptive, and beauty is fleeting; but a woman who fears the LORD is to be praised. Give her the reward she has earned, and let her works bring her praise at the city gate.

❊ **Your Turn:** Write or text a message back to God about your life, what you read, or a request on your heart:

_____

_____

_____

_____

LOL

Strong-Willed Communication

Kendra Smiley, author of *Journey of a Strong-Willed Child*, gives a picture of the smiles a strong-willed child can create:

My strong-willed son was about 12 years old. He was debating with me, and I decided the debate should end. I picked up a tablet and pointed to the side of it.

"This is the edge," I said. Then I placed my finger very close to that same side and said, "This is your mother. You'll notice that I'm very close to the edge."

With that he went to his room and closed the door behind him. I wondered if I had communicated my feelings well enough but was soon reassured when I overheard him telling his brothers, "Don't go out there. Mom's tense!"[2]

---

1. From "The Mavens' Word of the Day," Words@Random, November 14, 1996, s.v. "Beside oneself," www.randomhouse.com/wotd/index.pperl?date=19961114 (accessed March 16, 2010).
2. Kendra Smiley, personal story shared with authors. Used by permission.

The Faithful Rock

Text Message: *4 t Lᴏʀᴅ God is n evrlstng Rck.* *

Arlene Pellicane has a box she doesn't open often. It contains a photograph of a baby's feet, a tiny hospital wristband, and a small white dress with two pink satin roses at the top. Arlene's unborn baby had terrible chromosomal defects, and Arlene's gynecologist told her the baby would probably die in the womb. A specialist confirmed that the baby's heart would stop beating within two weeks. Heartbroken, Arlene tried to enjoy that Thanksgiving at church. When she went forward to pray, a woman met her and looked deep into her eyes. "God is faithful," the woman said—words that both pierced and comforted Arlene's heart. Claiming Proverbs 3:5-6, Arlene chose to trust God through those difficult days.

Her baby was still moving at Christmas, and Arlene wrote in her journal, "God gave us His Son at Christmas, and we give Him our daughter." Three days later, when her baby's heart stopped beating, Arlene knew her little girl, Angel Rose, was already safe in the arms of Jesus. As she went into labor to deliver the baby's body, she sensed God's presence.

The next spring, on the baby's due date, Arlene took a pregnancy test. It was positive, and nine months later she gave birth to a healthy baby girl, Noelle Joy. The next Christmas, she held her precious treasure and rejoiced: "One girl in heaven and one girl on earth," she said. Angel Rose taught Arlene that God is faithful—a Rock in times of struggle as well as times of joy.[1]

Do you need Jesus to be your Rock? A strong, sure place of refuge? In Bible times, those who referred to God as their Rock considered Him a place of refuge and safety above the battles of life.

---

* *So trust in the* Lord *(commit yourself to Him, lean on Him, hope confidently in Him) forever; for the* Lord *God is an everlasting Rock [the Rock of Ages].* (Isaiah 26:4, ᴀᴍᴘ)

Pick up a stone today and place it on your desk or windowsill to remind you that God is your Rock.

❋ **Send Up a Message:** Whether I'm going through times of pain or times of blessing, teach me to trust You, Father. Amen.

❋ **Text Helps:** Trust comes with learning more about a trustworthy God and experiencing His faithfulness firsthand. The following verses remind us that God is faithful and trustworthy. Memorize one of these verses today:

DEUTERONOMY 7:9—Know therefore that the LORD your God is God; he is the faithful God, keeping his covenant of love to a thousand generations of those who love him and keep his commands.

PSALM 9:10—Those who know your name will trust in you, for you, LORD, have never forsaken those who seek you.

PSALM 18:2, 31—The LORD is my rock, my fortress and my deliverer; my God is my rock, in whom I take refuge. He is my shield and the horn of my salvation, my stronghold. . . . For who is God besides the LORD? And who is the Rock except our God?

PSALM 46:1—God is our refuge and strength, an ever-present help in trouble.

❋ **Your Turn:** Write or text a message back to God about your life, what you read, or a request on your heart:

_____

_____

_____

_____

_____

_____

_____

LOL

Let's Take Good Care of God

Melanie Bell sent a funny story to *Today's Christian Woman*:

> My daughter, Laura, went with me to buy some grape juice for our church's communion service. Telling her it was for the Lord's Supper, I placed it in the refrigerator.
>
> Later, her older brother, Jonathan, saw it and wanted some. Laura scolded, "No, that's for God's lunch!"[2]

---

1. Arlene Pellicane, personal story shared with authors. Used by permission. Visit Arlene's Web site www.LosingWeightAfterBaby.com for more information.
2. Melanie Bell, article originally published in *Today's Christian Woman* (January–February 1996): 25; quoted in Pam Farrel, *Celebrate! I Made a Big Decision* (Colorado Springs: Chariot Victor, 2000), 16.

Better Than Chatty Cathy

Text Message: *"Lk! I m cmng qukly & my rwrd s wth me."**

Reel-to-reel tape recorders, Tinkertoys, Lincoln Logs, Jiffy Pop, and a Brownie camera—these are some of the things I [Dawn] just had to have as a young girl. (Yes, I know that dates me.) I remember thinking I'd almost die if I didn't get a Chatty Cathy doll for Christmas! But eventually, the things I thought were so valuable ended up lying on shelves or stuffed in Goodwill boxes. I thought I'd learned my lesson that things don't satisfy for long, but even as an adult, I collected Cherished Teddies figurines. Now I can't even give them away at a garage sale!

Only what is connected to God and His values will last. The Word of God will stand forever, and those we love who have new life in Christ will join us in heaven. Why don't we focus on these "everlasting" things?

The Bible gives us many examples of people who focused on something they desired—something that satisfied temporarily—and they ended up in sin, or worse.

It started with Eve (Genesis 3:6). Her disobedience resulted in dire consequences for not only her, but the rest of us as well. Lust for temporal satisfaction is found in Esau (Genesis 25:29-34), who sold his inheritance for a cup of soup. David's affair with Bathsheba (2 Samuel 11:1-4) created some dysfunctional kids. Achan's disobedience (Joshua 7)—trying to gain illegal goods—led to his death. The selfishness of Ananias and Sapphira (Acts 5:1-10), as they held back financially and lied about it, resulted in God ending their lives.

These were all poor short-term choices with negative long-term consequences.

---

* *Look! I [Jesus] am coming quickly, and My reward is with Me to repay each person according to what he has done.* (Revelation 22:12, HCSB)

In contrast, Moses turned his back on the pleasures and treasures of Egypt, looking instead for an eternal reward (Hebrews 11:24-27). He is noted by God in the Hall of Faith as a model for all to follow. Even Jesus set aside His heavenly glory to come to earth to die for our sins (Philippians 2:6-7)—and the payoff? A heaven filled with those He loves, like you and me!

We have to remember that there are crowns to be won and rewards that will never pass away! They are profoundly better than earthly treasures, even a Chatty Cathy. Follow Christ's example; God's glory and gifts of reward await you.

Dawn and I [Pam] have a friend, Ken Nichols, who named his ministry the way he thinks and lives: ALIVE—Always Living In Light of Eternity.[1] Be ALIVE! Look at life through the eyes of eternity and make your choices for lasting impact.

❀ **Send Up a Message:** Give me wisdom, Lord, to seek Your eternal perspective. Amen.

❀ **Text Helps:** Read a few of the stories about the Bible characters mentioned earlier in this chapter and the positive and negative choices they made. Have you also made some choices that had negative consequences? God forgives and still can use us, but He wants us to have His perspective. Consider the following scriptures as you commit to making better choices in the days ahead.

1 CORINTHIANS 2:9—No eye has seen, no ear has heard, no mind has conceived what God has prepared for those who love him.

GALATIANS 1:10—Am I now trying to win the approval of men, or of God? Or am I trying to please men? If I were still trying to please men, I would not be a servant of Christ.

❀ **Your Turn:** Write or text a message back to God about your life, what you read, or a request on your heart:

_____

_____

_____

LOL

All Bran, Baby!

An 85-year-old couple, having been married almost 60 years, died in a car crash. They had been in good health the past 10 years, mainly due to the wife's interest in health food and exercise.

When they reached the pearly gates, Saint Peter took them to their mansion, which was decked out with a beautiful kitchen, a master-bath suite, and a Jacuzzi. As they "oohed and aahed," the old man asked Peter how much all this was going to cost.

"It's free," Peter replied. "This is heaven."

Next they went out back to see the championship golf course behind the house. They would have golfing privileges every day, and each week the course changed to a new one representing the great golf courses on earth.

The old man asked, "What are the green fees?"

Peter's reply: "This is heaven; you play for free."

Next they went to the clubhouse and saw a lavish buffet lunch with the cuisines of the world laid out before them.

"How much to eat?" asked the old man.

"Don't you understand yet? This is heaven. It's free!" Peter replied.

"Well, where are the low-fat, low-cholesterol foods?" the old man asked timidly.

"That's the best part. You can eat as much as you like of whatever you like, and you never get fat and you never get sick. This is heaven."

The old man looked at his wife and said, "You and your bran muffins. I could have been here 10 years ago!"[2]

---

1. To learn more about Alive Ministries, visit Ken Nichols's Web site at www. aliveministries.net/.
2. Original source unknown. Adapted from "It's All Free," Heaven Jokes, Jokes About Network, www.jokesaboutheaven.com/heaven_jokes_three.html (accessed March 16, 2010).

Just Right

Text Message: *D Lᴏʀᴅ lks @ d hrt.* *

"I'm too young," some people say. "God can't use me," others claim. "I'm too old!" They sound like Goldilocks complaining about her porridge: "Too hot; too cold." But remember, with a new choice Goldilocks found the perfect porridge—"just right."

Renee Johnson, 25, saturated her life with the Word of God but realized that many of her friends didn't have the same love for the Bible. Renee didn't let her youth stand in the way. She became an online "Devotional Diva," encouraging her 20-something friends with a practical application of Scripture, and within a year she was contacted by a publisher to write a book to reach her generation![1]

In contrast, Evelyn Gregory, retiring from banking after the death of her husband, decided to pursue her childhood dream of being a flight attendant. After several airlines rejected her, Evelyn was hired by US Airways Express. She served people as a flight attendant until she was 77.[2]

I [Dawn] only completed two years of college in my 20s, but I returned to finish my degree as I turned 50! I wanted the Lord to expand my horizons of ministry. Perhaps God wants to use your spiritual gifts in a new way. He may want you to offer your financial resources, to open your home, to invest in a younger person's life, or to help someone make better choices. It really doesn't matter how old you are—what matters is, are you eager to be used?

Young, old, or in between, you are "just right" for God to use *right now*. God used young Esther to save her people (Esther 8:1-17), courageous Deborah to motivate God's warriors (Judges 4:4-24), and wise old Elizabeth to shelter and encourage young Mary (Luke 1:41-56). Each

---

* *Man looks at the outward appearance, but the* Lᴏʀᴅ *looks at the heart.* (1 Samuel 16:7)

woman turned divine interruptions into ministry opportunities, embracing God's direction with hope and faith.

The Lord can use anyone who offers Him a pure, willing heart. He only asks us to do what we can at any age. How can you use *your* gifts? I [Pam] recently saw a billboard in an airport with a picture of 90-year-old skier Klaus Obermeyer. I also saw a video on the Internet of 91-year-old water-skier Edith McAllister. If these two can ski after 90, you, too, can use your talent, skill, wisdom, and experience in a way to encourage, build up, or equip someone in some way today to make the world a better place! So, get out of the boat and into the water. Make a difference today!

❊ **Send Up a Message:** Heavenly Father, I'm so grateful that You can use us at any age. Show me how I can serve You today. Amen.

❊ **Text Helps:** Read the stories of Esther (Esther 8:1-17), Deborah (Judges 4:4-24), and Elizabeth (Luke 1:39-56)—three women God used in different seasons of life. Then read the following scriptures and open your heart to God using you, too.

PSALM 40:8—I desire to do your will, O my God; your law is within my heart.

MARK 14:8-9—[Jesus said,] "She did what she could. She poured perfume on my body beforehand to prepare for my burial. I tell you the truth, wherever the gospel is preached throughout the world, what she has done will also be told, in memory of her."

❊ **Your Turn:** Write or text a message back to God about your life, what you read, or a request on your heart:

_____

_____

_____

_____

_____

LOL

Waiting to Turn Four

Kendra Smiley, author of *Be the Parent,* shares a story from her travels:

> I was waiting at the airport gate for my flight to board. It was a long wait, and a mother and her four-year-old daughter were sitting near me.
>
> Before long we struck up a conversation. I asked the little girl how old she was.
>
> "Four," she replied quickly. And then she turned to me, and in a hushed tone, she added, "They made me say three for a really long time!"[3]

---

1. Visit Renee Johnson's Web site at www.devotionaldiva.com.
2. The story of Evelyn Gregory, presented in Prill Boyle, *Defying Gravity: A Celebration of Late-Blooming Women* (Cincinnati: Clerisy Press, 2005), www.prillboyle.com/women/evelyngregory.html (accessed March 16, 2010).
3. Kendra Smiley, personal story shared with authors. Used by permission.

Camp Grammy

Text Message: *Chldrn r a hritg fr t Lord.* *

I [Dawn] never expected to be so busy in my 50s. I had always imagined I'd be just like my grandma Parks—sewing and baking cookies. But God had other plans: college at age 50, a new ministry at 56, and a crazy-packed writing and speaking calendar. These days I find that I have to be proactive and schedule in time for my granddaughters.

Schedule them in? That sounds horrible, but it's my reality. The point is, I care about these precious girls, and I want to be a part of their lives whenever I can.

One October I planned a "Camp Grammy." I cleared away all the breakables from the living room and gave Megan and Jenna blankets and clothespins. We designed a "campground," draping the blankets over chairs, a small table, and the coffee table. We added a large American flag, turned out the lights, turned on flashlights, and crawled into our "tent" to tell stories and eat microwaved s'mores.

We giggled and laughed, and I told them how much I love them. I told them God has wonderful plans for their lives, and we prayed for their husbands, growing up somewhere in the world.

Children and grandchildren are indeed our heritage from God. I want to help my grandchildren root themselves in the Word of God and soar in His purposes for their lives. My granddaughters may not remember "Camp Grammy" when they're older, but I will always cherish the time I spent with them. And I hope they will never forget that their Grammy loves them and prays for them.

---

* *Behold, children are a heritage from the* Lord, *the fruit of the womb is a reward.* (Psalm 127:3, NKJV)

If you have grandchildren (or children still living in your home, or you're an 'auntie'), be intentional about pointing them to the Lord. Think for a moment about how you've influenced them so far. Do you need to make any changes from this point on? Even if you're not a grandparent right now, you can still create God-ward memories to bless your family, co-workers, and friends.

✳ **Send Up a Message:** Give me a godly heritage, Father. Help me teach my family Your ways. Amen.

✳ **Text Helps:** The most important thing you can pass on to future generations is knowledge of God—who He is and what He has done for us in His Son, Jesus. Help the children around you catch a vision of the Lord. Let the following verses motivate you!

PSALM 103:17—From everlasting to everlasting the LORD's love is with those who fear him, and his righteousness with their children's children.

PSALM 127:3—Sons are a heritage from the LORD, children a reward from him.

ISAIAH 44:3—I [the Lord] will pour out my Spirit on your offspring, and my blessing on your descendants.

✳ **Your Turn:** Write or text a message back to God about your life, what you read, or a request on your heart:

_____

_____

_____

_____

_____

_____

_____

_____

_____

_____

LOL

The Grandma Test

Have you ever heard about the "Grandma Test"? A grandmother told this story:

I was out walking with my four-year-old granddaughter. She picked up something off the ground and started to put it in her mouth. I took the item away from her and asked her not to do that.

"Why?" my granddaughter asked.

"Because it's been on the ground. You don't know where it's been, it's dirty, and probably has germs," I replied.

At this point, my granddaughter looked at me with total admiration and asked, "Grandma, how do you know all this stuff? You are so smart."

I was thinking quickly, "All grandmas know this stuff. It's on the Grandma Test. You have to know it, or they don't let you be a grandma."

We walked along in silence for two or three minutes, but she was evidently pondering this new information.

"Oh . . . I get it!" she beamed. "So if you don't pass the test, you have to be the grandpa."

"Exactly," I replied.[1]

---

1. Original source unknown. Quoted in "The Grandma Test," Cybersalt Communications, www.cybersalt.org/cleanlaugh-archive/4067-the-grandma-test (accessed March 16, 2010).

Crazy Love

Text Message: *Movd w cmpssn, Jesus strchd ot Hs hnd.* *

Many families struggle with mental illness. In fact, "about one in five Americans experiences a mental disorder in a given year. This represents about 44 million people."[1] In our [the Farrel] family, we also have someone in our extended family who struggles with paranoia, is often paralyzed by fear, and has a form of agoraphobia (fear of leaving one's home). (However, she isn't a harm to herself or others in a way that the law would allow us to intervene.) Because of this, she lives in her own reality, so we don't have what you would call a "normal" relationship with her. But we've worked hard to create an ongoing relationship with her because we long to show Christ's love to her.

Sometimes her reality is a little outrageous. She might want us all to dress up in *Nutcracker* ballet outfits to go out to dinner. (Ah, yeah . . . not really something our three teenage sons were excited about! LOL.)

We've set up a few traditions that have helped maintain the relationship:

1. Knowing she is agitated if guests are around more than 90 minutes, we have an "85-minute-visit" rule so she won't behave in an unkind or unreasonable way toward those who might misunderstand or see her behavior as unloving.

2. We maintain control of the environment. That means we drive our car, we always have a plan B, and so on.

3. We have educated everyone in her world about her history, so people can have compassion rather than becoming offended or frustrated when trying to relate to her.

4. We love her for what she can give, not for what she is unable to give. We have released her from our own expectations and simply love her unconditionally.

---

* *Moved with compassion, Jesus stretched out His hand.* (Mark 1:41, NASB)

5. We hold out tangible help to her, so if she is ever willing, help can be mobilized.

6. We don't take responsibility for her unwillingness to accept help or judge ourselves because of her resistance. We give ourselves the same unconditional love we believe God wants us to extend to her.

7. We keep a sense of humor. If we're in our home or hers—not in public—we all might play the board game Operation (made for younger children) that she gave to our 21-year-old, or we'll wear the clown hats she created for my 40th birthday. If it's harmless and doesn't enable her controlling behaviors, we just laugh and love her through the experience.

Boundaries help protect the relationship and give God time to work on the person in need. Loving unconditionally keeps our hearts soft while we're waiting, so that when God does work, there will be a relationship for the formerly (or currently) mentally ill to experience. "Eccentric" humor can actually help you laugh out loud, if you relax and enjoy it. Just ask our 21-year-old wearing the clown hat and winning at Operation.

❉ **Send Up a Message:** Lord, help me to love others unconditionally and know when to step in and help. Amen.

❉ **Text Helps:** Everyone has someone in his or her life who can be difficult to love. Read the following verses for some insight on how to be filled with God's love when you aren't feeling it.

MATTHEW 9:36—Seeing the people, [Jesus] felt compassion for them, because they were distressed and dispirited like sheep without a shepherd. (NASB)

MARK 6:34—When Jesus landed and saw a large crowd, he had compassion on them, because they were like sheep without a shepherd. So he began teaching them many things.

❉ **Your Turn:** Write or text a message back to God about your life, what you read, or a request on your heart:

_____

_____

LOL

Forgetfulness

A man looked a little worried when the doctor came in to administer his annual physical, so the first thing the doctor did was to ask whether anything was troubling him.

"Well, to tell the truth, Doc, yes," answered the patient. "You see, I seem to be getting forgetful. No, it's actually worse than that. I'm never sure I can remember where I put the car, or whether I answered a letter, or where I'm going, or what it is I'm going to do once I get there—if I get there. So, I really need your help. What can I do?"

The doctor mused for a moment, [and] then answered in his kindest tone, "Pay me in advance."[2]

There can be an upside for the patient, too . . .

An agitated patient was stomping around the psychiatrist's office, running his hands through his hair, almost in tears.

"Doctor, my memory's gone. Gone! I can't remember my wife's name. Can't remember my children's names. Can't remember what kind of car I drive. Can't remember where I work. It was all I could do to find my way here!"

"Calm down, sir! How long have you been like this?"

"Like what?"[3]

---

1. U.S. Department of Health and Human Services, *Surgeon General's Report on Mental Health* (Washington, DC: Government Printing Office, 1999), cited in L. Jans, S. Stoddard, and L. Krause, U.S. Department of Education, National Institute on Disability and Rehabilitation Research, *Chartbook on Mental Health and Disability*, Infouse Project (Washington DC: Government Printing Office, 2004), www.infouse.com/disabilitydata/mentalhealth/1_1.php.

2. Original source unknown. Quoted in "Losing His Memory," Clean Doctor Jokes, ChristiansUnite.com, http://jokes.christiansunite.com/Doctors/Losing_His_Memory.shtml (accessed March 16, 2010).

3. Original source unknown. Quoted in "Losing My Mind," Jokes and Fun, www.joomlaspan.com/fun/jokes/13023/Losing_my_mind!.html (accessed March 16, 2010).

Ready to Snap!

Text Message: *Gr8 pc hv they who lv Yr lw.* *

A friend once sent me [Dawn] "36 Christian Ways to Reduce Stress." The list included many practical suggestions, such as "go to bed on time," "simplify and unclutter your life," and "live within your budget." But the suggestion that really made me laugh was this one: "Remind yourself that you are not the General Manager of the Universe!"[1]

Women often suffer from "hurry sickness" and "control mania," and it leads to burnout! Psychiatrist Edward Hallowell, author of *Crazy Busy: Overstretched, Overbooked, and About to Snap,*[2] says he knew he had crossed into the "dark side" of stress when he got frustrated with a rotary phone while on vacation. Unable to use his cell phone in the vacation house, he grew tense waiting for the phone dial to return to its original position after dialing each digit!

In this fast-paced world and busy to the max—I hate to admit this—I'm often ready to snap when faced with unexpected circumstances or interruptions. I leave too little cushion time. A loving accountability partner paraphrased a Bible verse for me as a remedy for my overwhelmed life. "God," she wrote, "wants you to cease striving and know Him" (Psalm 46:10). "He wants you to stop running in anxious circles and take time to connect with His Word."

I took her advice and enjoyed the wonderful blessings that flow from God's presence—peace, provision, and power. We're so used to being busy that sometimes it can be difficult to slow down and make changes in our lives. Do you ever find yourself ready to snap? I want to encourage you to take a few moments today and just slow down. Close

---

* *Great peace have they who love your law, and nothing can make them stumble.* (Psalm 119:165)

your eyes. Breathe deeply. Spend quiet time in prayer.

I [Pam] wrote a chapter in *The 10 Best Decisions a Woman Can Make*[3] originally titled "What to Do When You Are Sick and Tired of Being Sick and Tired." In it I encouraged readers, "Care for yourself so you can care for *the rest* of your life." One of the best ways to care for ourselves is to remember that God is in charge, not us!

❋ **Send Up a Message:** Father, I worry about many things, struggling and running around in circles when I should sit at Your feet instead. Teach me to seek Your Word sooner. Amen.

❋ **Text Helps:** Are you rushing around today, maybe even rushing through this time with the Lord? Take a deep breath. Then be still and focus on the Lord to sense His peace, as these verses suggest:

PSALM 46:10—Be still, and know that I am God; I will be exalted among the nations, I will be exalted in the earth.

ISAIAH 48:18—If only you had paid attention to my commands, your peace would have been like a river, your righteousness like the waves of the sea.

LUKE 10:38-42—As Jesus and his disciples were on their way, he came to a village where a woman named Martha opened her home to him. She had a sister called Mary, who sat at the Lord's feet listening to what he said. But Martha was distracted by all the preparations that had to be made. She came to him and asked, "Lord, don't you care that my sister has left me to do the work by myself? Tell her to help me!" "Martha, Martha," the Lord answered, "you are worried and upset about many things, but only one thing is needed. Mary has chosen what is better, and it will not be taken away from her."

❋ **Your Turn:** Write or text a message back to God about your life, what you read, or a request on your heart:

_____

_____

_____

LOL

Talk About Controlling!

A husband and wife accompanied their son and his fiancée when they met with her pastor to sign some pre-wedding ceremony papers. While filling out the form, their son read aloud a few questions.

When he got to the last one, which read, "Are you entering this marriage at your own will?" he looked over at his fiancée.

"Put down 'yes,'" she said.[4]

1. Original source unknown. Quoted in "36 Christian Ways to Reduce Stress," Heart4Home.net, www.heart4home.net/downloads/reduce_stress.pdf (accessed March 16, 2010).
2. Edward M. Hallowell, *Crazy Busy: Overstretched, Overbooked, and About to Snap!* (New York: Ballantine Books, 2006).
3. Pam Farrel, *The 10 Best Decisions a Woman Can Make* (Eugene, OR: Harvest House, 2004).
4. Lilyan Van Almeto, "Forced into It," Joke of the Day, *Reader's Digest*, June 24, 2009.

Perch and Rest

Text Message: *"I wl gv u rst."**

If you're like most women, you've already got a full to-do list—there's no room for something like rest! But the truth is that we need rest, and God wants to give us the peace we need to slow down.

My [Dawn's] friend Corrie Bush is an excellent example of someone who learned that God wanted to help her stop and rest.[1] Sadly, she was molested as a child and grew up in fear, with a desire to run from life. Corrie ran to the streets into the arms of strangers, drugs, and drink. Alcohol still had a grip on her life when she met her husband at age 21. She knew that as an alcoholic, she couldn't lead her husband to Christ, so she began a long, painful process of healing from the scars of her life. Overwhelmed by God's love, she surrendered to Him, and yet scars remained.

In the midst of her healing, Corrie was amazed to see one hummingbird after another, everywhere she went. Hummingbirds can perch, but they don't walk. They also don't flap their wings. They fly by moving their tiny wrist bones—their "hands"—at 38 to 78 strokes per second. They scurry around in all directions, rotating 180 degrees. Their resting heartbeat is 480 beats per minute, but their hearts can beat as fast as 1,260 times per minute when they're excited![2] Just *thinking* about that makes me tired! Sometimes hummingbirds simply need to perch for a while.

"Hummingbirds," Corrie said, "remind me of how desperate I am for rest—how desperate I am for my Maker to still my heart. It's as if God says, 'Be still, my little hummingbird.'"

Oh, how we need to hear those words. We scurry around doing many good things, but we get worn out and tired. We desperately need

---

* [Jesus said,] *"Come to me, all you who are weary and burdened, and I will give you rest."* (Matthew 11:28)

the presence and Word of God. If we listen, we'll hear God say, "Dear one, perch and rest, and you'll accomplish more in a little while."

Understanding this need, the psalmist wrote, "Oh, that I had wings like a dove! I would fly away and be at rest" (Psalm 55:6, NKJV). In Psalm 37:7, we are encouraged to "rest in the LORD, and wait patiently for him" (NKJV). Church leader Charles Wesley explained it this way: "Do not repine [complain] at [God's] dealings, but quietly submit to his will, and wait for his help."[3]

Today, do something radical—rest! Take a nap, take five minutes to sit or lie in the sun, relax to your favorite music, thumb through a magazine, climb into a hammock and pray, or slip into a bubble bath or Jacuzzi for a soak. Stop for at least five minutes for a few deep breaths! When you pause, roll your stressors into Jesus' arms and off your shoulders, knowing that the Lord of all will take *care* of it all. When you're refreshed, God will likely show you your part of the assignment. It will feel more doable after you rest in His arms of love.

❊ **Send Up a Message:** Help me rest in Your presence, Father, strengthened by Your Word. Amen.

❊ **Text Helps:** God's presence is the place of rest, and His desire is to give you rest. As you read the following verses, think of ways you can rest in Him today.

PSALM 37:7—Rest in the LORD, and wait patiently for Him; do not fret because of him who prospers in his way, because of the man who carries out wicked schemes. (NASB)

ISAIAH 30:15—This is what the Sovereign LORD, the Holy One of Israel, says: "In repentance and rest is your salvation, in quietness and trust is your strength, but you would have none of it."

❊ **Your Turn:** Write or text a message back to God about your life, what you read, or a request on your heart:

_____

_____

_____

LOL

When Life Gets a Little Out-of-Control

A friend of ours shared this story with us:

My mom, Blanca Brumble, was pregnant with her third child at the age of 39. She was also a full-time teacher, wife to a policeman, and mother to two other daughters. Balancing all that—along with her raging hormones—was a challenge to say the least!

One morning she was rushing to school for an early teachers' meeting. After jumping out of our minivan, waving hello to some of the high-school boys in the parking lot, and then running up the stairs to the office, she paused, knowing she had forgotten something. "I left my skirt at home!" she cried out. Luckily she was wearing a black slip so it wasn't *completely* obvious. Everyone burst out laughing, including my mom, before she rushed home to put the rest of her clothes on!

Just a few weeks later, my mom (still pregnant) and I were riding with some friends to a special banquet dinner. My mom was in the passenger seat up front. Suddenly, she leaned over and started laughing.

"I'm wearing two dresses!" In our rush to get ready after school for the banquet that evening, my mother had pulled on her dress without thinking to take off the other one. My mom and her friend couldn't stop giggling, and pretty soon we were all laughing out loud.[4]

---

1. Corrie Bush, personal correspondence with authors, April 1, 2009. Used by permission.
2. "All You Want to Know," Hummingbird Facts and Information, Hummingbirds, www.mschloe.com/hummer/huminfo.htm (accessed March 16, 2010).
3. Charles Wesley, quoted in "Wesley's Notes on the Bible," Biblos.com, s.v. "Psalm 37," http://wes.biblecommenter.com/psalms/37.htm.
4. Blanca Brumble's personal story. Used by permission.

Four J's for Our Trials

Text Message: *B jyfl n hope,*
patnt n aflikn, fthfl n pryr. *

The Bible is filled with examples of how to bear up under trials and afflictions in life. One woman and three men, in particular, demonstrated an unwavering faith in God in difficult circumstances—and all their names start with the letter *J*.

Jochebed, Moses' mother, launched her little one onto the Nile River in a handcrafted cradle to spare his life, her hopes fastened securely to the protecting hand of God (Exodus 1:22–2:3).

Job showed incredible insight and patience after he lost his children, his cattle, and his health. He didn't fall apart but turned to worship God with unshakable confidence (Job 19:25).

Joseph suffered at the hands of his brothers and a captain's wife in Egypt, enduring both a pit and prison. But he learned to trust God for the things he didn't understand, and he acknowledged the sovereign purposes of God (Genesis 37–50; 50:20).

Jesus endured the cross following a prayerful night of surrender in Gethsemane. He suffered not only scoffing, persecution, and horrible physical pain at the hands of those who condemned Him to die, but He also bore our sins in His sinless body (2 Corinthians 5:21). He endured it all for the sure hope of our salvation (Romans 5:8; Hebrews 12:2).

All of these and many others in the Bible endured life's afflictions with hearts firmly trusting in God. The word *endure* means "to hold up; to hold oneself erect; to stand." Sometimes it is victory to just rise up and stand. These people are wonderful examples of those who

---

* *Be joyful in hope, patient in affliction, faithful in prayer.* (Romans 12:12)

chose to stand. Their faith and prayers led to joyful hope, patience, and faithfulness.

What struggle are you facing today, friend? Place your heart and hopes in the Father's hands . . . then *stand!*

✽ **Send Up a Message:** Thank You, Father, that I can come to You in all my struggles, knowing I can trust You. Teach me to be patient and prayerful in my trials. Amen.

✽ **Text Helps:** None of us will escape trials and struggles in life, but we have the Word of God and the example of Jesus to help us cope. Allow the following scriptures to help you fix your eyes on Him.

ROMANS 8:35-39—Who shall separate us from the love of Christ? Shall trouble or hardship or persecution or famine or nakedness or danger or sword? As it is written: "For your sake we face death all day long; we are considered as sheep to be slaughtered." No, in all these things we are more than conquerors through him who loved us. For I am convinced that neither death nor life, neither angels nor demons, neither the present nor the future, nor any powers, neither height nor depth, nor anything else in all creation, will be able to separate us from the love of God that is in Christ Jesus our Lord.

2 CORINTHIANS 4:8-11—We are hard pressed on every side, but not crushed; perplexed, but not in despair; persecuted, but not abandoned; struck down, but not destroyed. We always carry around in our body the death of Jesus, so that the life of Jesus may also be revealed in our body. For we who are alive are always being given over to death for Jesus' sake, so that his life may be revealed in our mortal body.

HEBREWS 12:2—Let us fix our eyes on Jesus, the author and perfecter of our faith, who for the joy set before him endured the cross.

✳ **Your Turn:** Write or text a message back to God about your life, what you read, or a request on your heart:

_____

_____

_____

_____

LOL

Wise Guys

Our friend Judy shared this true snapshot of how young people gather common sense:

> During my daughter Amy's world history class, they were discussing the days of Charlemagne in preparation for a pop quiz the following day.
> "During this era," the teacher lectured, "the code of chivalry placed the noble-women of the day on a pedestal, to be cherished and protected. Songs and poems glorifying these women and praising their beauty and gentleness were written by a certain group of men." Searching for the word *troubadour,* he asked, "What were these men called?"
> "Wise men," my high schooler dryly replied.[1]

---

1. Judy Scharfenberg, e-mail message to Dawn. Used by permission.

Got a Hold on You

Text Message: *Now t God o pce b w/ u all.* *

My [Pam's] two-year-old granddaughter reaches for my hand anytime we walk. Recently as we walked together, she heard the rumbling of a train nearby and, reaching up for me, said, "Eden scared. Eden scared."

She knows I'm there for her. She knows I will rescue her.

We are God's kids. He wants us to know that He is there for us. Sure, walking with God does have its payoffs. I have a happy marriage and three terrific sons who are smart, capable, giving citizens. I have amazing friendships, and I get to work doing what I love. I'm blessed to travel to many exciting places and meet some interesting, inspiring people. I have a safe home and enjoy the hope of heaven. But these aren't the reasons I believe in Jesus.

When I was in college, I discovered a thing called Christian music. I was introduced to an artist named Evie, who sang a song titled "If Heaven Was Never Promised to Me." The song caused me to ask, "Why *do* I believe in Jesus?"

Although everyone would answer this question differently, here's what my list looks like:

- God heard my cry for help when my abusive father was out of control.
- God walked me out of chaos through the wisdom of a godly mentor.
- God challenged me to rethink how to run a love relationship.
- God sent food supernaturally when Bill and I were struggling, poor students.
- God gave me a bicycle to ride when my car died.

---

* *The God of peace be with you all. Amen.* (Romans 15:33, NKJV)

- God gave Bill and me hope in the face of death, disease, and disappointments.
- God gave me wisdom when I was perplexed in my parenting.
- God gave me love when I was angry or frustrated in my marriage.
- God has always been with me.

I fell in love with my husband when he explained the meaning of a simple phrase on the front of his leather Bible—"That they may know You." This phrase comes from John 17:3: "Now this is eternal life: that they may know you, the only true God, and Jesus Christ, whom you have sent."

Eternal life means knowing God *now*, not waiting until heaven. To know Christ is to know the one called "Immanuel," which means, "God with us" (Matthew 1:23). It is to know the God who said, "Surely I am with you always, to the very end of the age" (Matthew 28:20). It is to know the God who promised, "I will never desert you, nor will I ever forsake you" (Hebrews 13:5, NASB).

Begin your own list of why you believe in Jesus here:

1. _____
2. _____
3. _____
4. _____
5. _____

Dawn and I don't know what this day holds for you, but we know the One who will hold you together through this day—Jesus. Just ask Him.

✳ **Send Up a Message:** Lord, thank You for walking with me today and every day—no matter what. Amen.

✳ **Text Helps:** God is *with* us! Is there a more powerful thought to bring us peace? Read these encouraging words and thank God for His presence in your life:

MATTHEW 1:22-23—All this took place to fulfill what the Lord had said through the prophet: "The virgin will be with child and will give birth to a son, and they will call him Immanuel"—which means, "God with us."

MATTHEW 28:18-20—Jesus came to [His disciples] and said, "All authority in heaven and on earth has been given to me. Therefore go and make disciples of all nations, baptizing them in the name of the Father and of the Son and of the Holy Spirit, and teaching them to obey everything I have commanded you. And surely I am with you always, to the very end of the age."

HEBREWS 13:5-6—God has said, "Never will I leave you; never will I forsake you." So we say with confidence, "The Lord is my helper; I will not be afraid. What can man do to me?"

❋ **Your Turn:** Write or text a message back to God about your life, what you read, or a request on your heart:

_____

_____

_____

_____

LOL

Wake Up!

My friend Gail and I [Pam] were sharing about the struggles we experience when we get calls from our grown kids, who live far away—calls that leave us struggling to offer words of encouragement.

Gail shared a story about a time she caught her own mother off guard. She lived in California at the time, and in the middle of the night, an earthquake hit, rattling windows, pushing books off shelves, knocking dishes out of cupboards, and even moving the bed across the room.

Frightened, Gail called her mom.

"Mom!" she said. "The dishes are falling! The bed is moving!"

To which her mother calmly replied, "Oh, honey, wake up! You're having a nightmare."

❋ ❋ ❋

God's Training Program

Text Message: *N do tm we wl rp.* *

My [Dawn's] young sons learned some important lessons as they watched *The Karate Kid* years ago. When young Daniel Larusso (played by Ralph Macchio) wanted to learn how to defend himself against bullies, his mentor, Mr. Miyagi (Pat Morita), offered unconventional "karate" lessons. He instructed Daniel to wash cars and complete other chores. Menial work. *Hard* work.

After each task, Mr. Miyagi simply advised, "Come back tomorrow."

Daniel, though frustrated, always came back. He hoped that the next lesson would be "real" training, not knowing that each of his chores included movements designed to prepare muscle memory for the defensive blocks of karate. Mr. Miyagi taught Daniel more than karate; he prepared the boy to face the struggles of life.[1]

With wisdom *far* beyond Mr. Miyagi's, God shapes our lives into the image of Christ. He gives us assignments that may seem menial, but each task is designed to make us holy and help us stand firm in battle against our Enemy. God teaches us to respond to tough circumstances with absolute trust in His purposes and to obey His instructions with the utmost care. This isn't always easy. It takes determination and practice on our part.

The truth is that God knows what He is doing. The trials He allows in our lives are meant to strengthen us, not defeat us. He knows the strength of the Enemy, and He wants us to be prepared. God also knows the weakness of our flesh, and He disciplines us so we'll rely on *His* strength. Our part is to do what is right and wait on Him in faith, not to grow weary in the process.

---

* *Let us not lose heart in doing good, for in due time we will reap if we do not grow weary.* (Galatians 6:9, NASB)

In an article about the necessity to put on our spiritual armor, Dr. David Jeremiah wrote, "God intends us to be 'more than conquerors,' but we have to be strong in the Lord and in the power of His might. Be dressed for battle, keep your armor on, and when it's all over but the shouting, you'll still be on your feet."[2]

Don't give up! God's training program is designed to bless you and glorify His name.

✳ **Send Up a Message:** Lord, help me embrace the lessons You teach. I depend on Your wisdom and grace. Amen.

✳ **Text Helps:** Is God calling you to discipline some area of your life? Listen to the counsel and teaching in these verses.

ISAIAH 40:31—Those who hope in the LORD will renew their strength. They will soar on wings like eagles; they will run and not grow weary, they will walk and not be faint.

2 CORINTHIANS 3:17-18—The Lord is the Spirit, and where the Spirit of the Lord is, there is freedom. And we, who with unveiled faces all reflect the Lord's glory, are being transformed into his likeness with ever-increasing glory, which comes from the Lord, who is the Spirit.

HEBREWS 12:1, 7, 11—Since we are surrounded by such a great cloud of witnesses, let us throw off everything that hinders and the sin that so easily entangles, and let us run with perseverance the race marked out for us. . . . Endure hardship as discipline; God is treating you as sons. For what son is not disciplined by his father? . . . No discipline seems pleasant at the time, but painful. Later on, however, it produces a harvest of righteousness and peace for those who have been trained by it.

✳ **Your Turn:** Write or text a message back to God about your life, what you read, or a request on your heart:

_____

_____

_____

LOL

Making Babies

Eight-year-old Susie came home from school and informed her mother that in class they had learned how to make babies.

The mother, rather shaken by the development, called the teacher to complain.

After listening to the mother complain for a few minutes, the teacher responded, "Did you ask her to explain how it is done?"

"No," said the mother.

"Then ask her and call me back," replied the teacher.

"So how *do* you make babies?" the mother asked her daughter.

"You drop the 'y,' and add 'ies.'"[3]

---

1. *The Karate Kid*, directed by John G. Avildsen (Delphi Films/Columbia Pictures, 1984).
2. Dr. David Jeremiah, "How can I prepare myself for spiritual battles?" excerpt from *Turning Points*. Article posted August 23, 2005, at Christianity.com, http://www.christianity.com/11543288/.
3. Original source unknown. Quoted in "How to Make Babies," EntertainmentForumOnline.com, www.entertainmentforumonline.com/MiscH.html (accessed March 16, 2010).

Rainbow Reality

Test Message: *God sd, . . . "I hv st my bow in t cloud & it shl b a sign."**

My [Pam's] friend Margaret shared a story that helped her remember the importance of childlike faith:

> My family was driving back to our home in La Pointe, Haiti, from the capital city. We were tired, and all four of us were ready for the 160-mile trip—already 10 hours on the road—to come to an end. There were only two more rivers to cross when the car started to shake. We lost the brakes on a mountain road. We all prayed that my husband, Kevin, could get the car to stop before we slid off the mountain road and into the ravine.
>
> Fortunately, Kevin was able to stop the car, albeit on the wrong side of the road. Thank God no one was coming in the other direction. The last "Tap Tap" of the day (a Haitian bus of sorts) was passing by. My daughters Jennifer (eight years old) and Martha and I raced after the bus. My shoe broke en route. We crammed ourselves into the bus, and my shoe was thrown to me as the Tap Tap began to move.
>
> This bus was a small Toyota pickup, which was already crammed with 15 passengers and five sacks of rice. The three of us squeezed into the single front seat and prayed that we would see Kevin again.
>
> The bus was hardly able to navigate the mountain roads.

---

* God said, "This is the sign of the covenant which I am making between Me and you and every living creature that is with you, for all successive generations; I have set My bow in the cloud, and it shall be for a sign." (Genesis 9:12-13, NASB)

When we approached a washed-out bridge, which was only three inches wider than the car, we knew it was time to claim the promises of God. Jennifer asked me if it was okay to pray out loud for her daddy and our safety—that God would give us some sign that her daddy would be safe and we would arrive home safely.

When she opened her eyes, she looked up into the sky and saw a full rainbow. She knew God had heard her prayer. But the trip wasn't over yet. This particular bus was only going to the town of Port-de-Paix, which was five miles from home. The driver asked for $50 to take us all the way home. I had $10 in my pocket. I knew we had no way to get home.

When we arrived at the end of the bus route in Port-de-Paix, we got out of the bus in the rain, in the pitch black of night. Holding my broken shoe, I had no idea what to do; so prayer was our only hope. We asked God to give us a rainbow in our hearts—to claim His promises.

A few minutes later, a car horn beeped behind us. The bus driver came back to give us a ride home—for only $10. Eventually, Kevin made it home as well.[1]

In Genesis 9, God gave a rainbow to assure the survivors on the ark that they were going to be safe. Place a rainbow on your desk, on your refrigerator, or someplace to remind *you* that God keeps His promises.

✺ **Send Up a Message:** Lord, give me the faith to believe the promises You give. Amen.

✺ **Text Helps:** A wonderful promise of Scripture is that nature may wither, but God's Word "stands forever" (Isaiah 40:8). That means that His promises stand forever, too! Read about Noah in Genesis 9:8-13 and then explore a few of the other promises God has given us in the following scriptures. Discover hope!

JOHN 6:37 *(Promise of Acceptance)*—[Jesus said,] "All that the Father gives me will come to me, and whoever comes to me I will never drive away."

JOHN 10:28 *(Promise of Eternal Life)*—[Jesus said,] "I give them eternal life, and they shall never perish; no one can snatch them out of my hand."

HEBREWS 13:5 *(Promise of God's Presence)*—God has said, "Never will I leave you; never will I forsake you."

JAMES 1:5 *(Promise of Wisdom)*—If any of you lacks wisdom, he should ask God, who gives generously to all without finding fault, and it will be given to him.

1 JOHN 1:9 *(Promise of Forgiveness)*—If we confess our sins, he is faithful and just and will forgive us our sins and purify us from all unrighteousness.

❋ **Your Turn:** Write or text a message back to God about your life, what you read, or a request on your heart:

_____

_____

_____

L O L

Playing House

A little girl and a little boy were at daycare one day. The girl, Sally, approached the boy and said, "Hey, Billy, want to play house?"

He said, "Sure! What do you want me to do?"

Sally replied, "I want you to communicate your feelings."

"Communicate my feelings?" said a bewildered Billy. "I have no idea what that means."

The little girl nodded and said, "Perfect. You can be the husband."[2]

❋ ❋ ❋

---

1. Personal story shared with authors. Used by permission.
2. Original source unknown. Adapted from "Playing House," Bag-O-Laughs, Grant's Graceland, August 17, 2000, www.grantsgraceland.org/bag2/phome.html (accessed March 16, 2010).

Infusion of Joy

Text Message: *Thr s a tm 2 laf.* *

Joy invades like a tiny bloom that pushes through a crack in tough cement.

With passion for revival in America's churches, Del Fehsenfeld Jr. founded Life Action Ministries in 1971. His life and ministry in churches was marked by Spirit-led heart searching, holy living, and earnest prayer for revival—all still desperately needed in our churches today. Just before Del died with a brain tumor, he mentioned to his friend Randy Rebold, president of Living Proof and Primary Focus ministries,[1] that he had two regrets in ministry. Del wished he had taught the team to express more love to one another, and he wished they'd all laughed more.[2]

Randy promised Del that he would carry that message to the team, if Del could not. Twenty years later, in August 2009 at a ministry team revival week, Randy kept his promise. Team members wept when Randy shared Del's words. They expressed their love to one another and laughed at Randy's crazy antics and stories. An infusion of joy electrified the chapel.

Throughout the gospel story, as Jesus reached out to cleanse the world of its awful sin sickness and heal humanity's brokenness, He created joy. How could He not? He came to make all things new. Humor was one of Jesus' ministry tools—a lubricant for the rough edges of life. Joy, part of the fruit and evidence of the Holy Spirit's presence in believers, is like a flashlight in the dark, scattering shadows.

Although there is no substitute for the hard work of soul searching and anguished prayer, joy brings balance to our lives—joy over the promises of God, joy in God's goodness and grace. There is a time to laugh!

Are you struggling with a heavy burden today? Create a Gratitude File, or a Happy File, or a Joy File—and fill it with reasons to rejoice.

---

* *There is a time for everything . . . a time to laugh.* (Ecclesiastes 3:1, 4)

Record the fingerprints of God's love in your life. To get you started, let go of bad memories and shame, because you are *not* condemned if you belong to Jesus (Romans 8:1)! Rejoice in God's presence (Psalm 16:11).

❀ **Send Up a Message:** Father, give me the gift of holy laughter today. Amen.

❀ **Text Helps:** Just as a tea bag placed in hot water changes it and infuses it with flavor, the presence of God can change a heart and infuse it with joy. As you read the following scriptures, let joy rise in your heart and put a smile on your face!

PSALM 16:11—You have made known to me the path of life; you will fill me with joy in your presence, with eternal pleasures at your right hand.

PSALM 68:3—May the righteous be glad and rejoice before God; may they be happy and joyful.

ISAIAH 55:12—You will go out in joy and be led forth in peace; the mountains and hills will burst into song before you, and all the trees of the field will clap their hands.

1 THESSALONIANS 5:16—Be joyful always.

❀ **Your Turn:** Write or text a message back to God about your life, what you read, or a request on your heart:

_____

_____

_____

_____

LOL

Kissing Air

Nancy Sebastian Meyer, an author and Christian communicator, shares how we all have our moments while growing up:

One day in kindergarten, I kissed a little boy on the playground. Later at nap time, the teacher called me up to her desk. She talked to the boy first and then to me. To me, she said, "Nancy, why did you kiss him?"

I replied, "I was kissing air, and he got in the way!"[3]

1. For more information about these ministries, visit Primary Focus at www.primaryfocus. org and Living Proof at http://livingproofsingers.org/.
2. Personal story shared with authors. Used by permission.
3. Nancy Sebastian Meyer, personal story shared with authors. Used by permission.

Jesus Loves ME!

Text Message: *He 1st lvd us.* *

When I [Dawn] traveled on the road with a ministry in my early 20s, in almost every church some sweet old lady would come up to me and say, "You look just like 'so-and-so.'" For many years, I felt I must have the most average-looking face in the world to look like so many people! I still get that comment today.

In fact, a woman in a swimming class recently came up to me and called me Sharon.

"No," I said, "I'm Dawn."

She looked at me hard and said, "Are you *sure?*"

Yes, I'm sure. My fingerprints remind me that I'm unique. My DNA is unique. God may love sister so-and-so, but I know He loves me, too.

God hates my sin, but He loved me so much, He sent His Son, Jesus, to pay for all my sins. God loved me first! His love is personal and specific. Yes, He loves the world, but He also loves *me*, His child.

Writer and Christian apologist Josh McDowell once said it wasn't all the evidence he collected for the resurrection and deity of Christ that brought him to salvation. "What motivated my belief," he said, "was the realization I had that . . . if I were the only person alive, Jesus still would have died for me."[1]

God loves us while we are still unlovely and imperfect, yet He draws us to His own dear heart. He draws YOU because He loves YOU. He made YOU—wonderful, unique, individual YOU. If you haven't made the decision to accept God's love in Jesus, pause and talk to God. Simply tell Him you want to know and experience this love.

---

* *We love Him [God] because He first loved us.* (1 John 4:19, NKJV)

If you know this personal love of Jesus, share this plan of God's love today with someone in your world.

✳ **Send Up a Message:** I'm so glad You love me, Father. You love *me*! Amen.

✳ **Text Helps:** As you read the following scriptures, pick one that speaks to your heart about the amazing love God desires to share with you. Then draw close to Him in prayer.

JEREMIAH 31:3—The LORD has appeared . . . to me, saying: "Yes, I have loved you with an everlasting love; therefore with loving-kindness I have drawn you." (NKJV)

JOHN 3:16-17—For God so loved the world that He gave His only begotten Son, that whoever believes in Him should not perish but have everlasting life. For God did not send His Son into the world to condemn the world, but that the world through Him might be saved. (NKJV)

ROMANS 5:8—God demonstrates His own love toward us, in that while we were still sinners, Christ died for us. (NKJV)

✳ **Your Turn:** Write or text a message back to God about your life, what you read, or a request on your heart:

_____

_____

_____

_____

LOL

Effective Diet

A woman was terribly overweight, so her doctor put her on a diet.

"I want you to eat regularly for two days, then skip a day, and repeat this procedure for two weeks. The next time I see you, you'll have lost at least five pounds."

When the woman returned, she shocked the doctor by losing nearly 20 pounds.

"Why, that's amazing!" the doctor said. "Did you follow my instructions?" The woman nodded.

"I'll tell you though, I thought I was going to drop dead that third day."

"From hunger, you mean?"

"No, from skipping."[2]

---

1. Christy Tennant, "Josh McDowell on Defending the Bible," *Bible Study Magazine* (November December 2008): 12.
2. Original source unknown. "Effective Diet," Comic Relief, Dottie's Weight Loss Zone, www.dwlz.com/Humor?comic18.html (accessed March 17, 2010).

Shattered, but Forgiven

Text Message: *4 U Lᴏʀᴅ r gd, & rdy 2 4gv.* *

Not long after my husband and I [Dawn] married, we visited Bob's sister, Janice, and her husband, Tom, for a fancy dinner. In a moment of silliness, we made a toast with sparkling cider, but Tom and I clanked our glasses too hard. My gold-edged goblet shattered. Horrified, I ran to their bedroom and locked myself in the closet. It seems silly now, but at the time I was afraid Janice wouldn't forgive me for breaking her lovely glassware. Janice was more than gracious, and I had no reason to doubt her forgiveness. The problem was all mine.

Through the years, I've sometimes had that same response to God, and believe me, I've shattered a lot more than glass in His sight. I've disobeyed His Word and will over and over again.

Gracious and merciful, God is my forgiving heavenly Father, but sometimes I lurk in the shadows of guilt, unwilling to *receive* His forgiveness. When I respond that way, I don't fully believe the truth about God's forgiveness. My enemy, Satan, is a persistent accuser (Revelation 12:10), and he delights in encouraging feelings of guilt. The truth is, as God's forgiven child, I stand before Him with nothing held against me—everything is forgiven (Ephesians 1:7). In Christ, I am holy in God's sight, no matter my feelings.

Are you struggling under a load of guilt? I [Pam] have seen firsthand that unwarranted shame and guilt are huge time wasters—they sidetrack women from their potential. So I encourage women to confront the source of their guilt head-on by following these steps:

---

* *For You, Lord, are good, and ready to forgive, and abundant in mercy to all those who call upon You.* (Psalm 86:5, ɴᴋᴊᴠ)

- *Confess it.* Own up to your sin or imperfection before God.
- *Amend it.* If you hurt someone, seek to make it right.
- *Forget it.* God has, so agree with Him and walk away from the past.
- *Move forward.* Decide to purposefully press forward in a new, better way of life.

God doesn't want us to live under the weight of guilt. The response of faith is to believe Him and receive His forgiveness.

✳ **Send Up a Message:** Father, thank You for Your complete forgiveness because of Jesus' sacrifice for my sin. I am free from the burden of guilt! Amen.

✳ **Text Helps:** We are all broken people, and only God can put us back together again. When we agree with Him that we have sinned, He forgives us and changes our hearts. Forgiveness is the beginning of freedom and holiness, as these scriptures illustrate:

PSALM 103:10-13—[God] does not treat us as our sins deserve or repay us according to our iniquities. For as high as the heavens are above the earth, so great is his love for those who fear him; as far as the east is from the west, so far has he removed our transgressions from us. As a father has compassion on his children, so the LORD has compassion on those who fear him.

EPHESIANS 1:7—In him [Christ] we have redemption through his blood, the forgiveness of sins, in accordance with the riches of God's grace.

1 JOHN 1:7, 9—If we walk in the light, as he is in the light, we have fellowship with one another, and the blood of Jesus, his Son, purifies us from all sin. . . . If we confess our sins, he is faithful and just and will forgive us our sins and purify us from all unrighteousness.

※ **Your Turn:** Write or text a message back to God about your life, what you read, or a request on your heart:

_____

_____

_____

_____

_____

LOL

I Wanna Preach!

After church on a Sunday morning, a young boy suddenly announced to his mother, "Mom, I have decided I want to be a minister when I grow up."

"That's okay with us," the mother replied, "but what made you want to be a pastor?"

"Well," the boy replied, "I'll have to go to church on Sunday anyway, and I figure it will be more fun to stand up and yell than to sit still and listen."[1]

---

1. J. Otis and Gail Ledbetter, *Family Fragrance: Practical, Intentional Ways to Fill Your Home with the Aroma of Love* (Colorado Springs: Chariot Victor, 1998), 45.

The Mulligan

Text Message: *God dmonstr8s His own luv 2ward s.***

A mulligan is a do-over in golf. When you make a bad shot and want to restart, you take a mulligan and try again. Nobody really knows how the mulligan acquired its name. There are several possible origins, according to the United States Golf Association Museum. In one scenario, "a fellow by the name of David Mulligan frequented St. Lambert Country Club in Montreal, Quebec, during the 1920s. Mulligan let [a shot] rip off the tee one day, wasn't happy with the results, re-teed, and hit again. According to the story, he called it a 'correction shot,' but his partners thought a better name was needed and dubbed it a 'mulligan.'"[1]

Many of us need mulligans in life. Often, teens and young adults need mulligans as they launch out in life. We [Pam and Bill] give our children grace, or a mulligan, if needed as they struggle to own their lives.

One of our sons used his mulligan when he "forgot" to put water in the radiator after being reminded numerous times. He burned up his car engine, making it undrivable. This son went from driving a cool sports car to driving the only vehicle available, a full-size, used cargo van—very uncool.

Another son called in his mulligan when he had to retake two classes his freshman year. (We didn't get angry. We forgave him and then reminded him of the Farrel Family Scholarship fine print: We don't pay for round two of classwork. Mulligan means forgiveness, not enabling codependence.)

Still another child used the mulligan to change colleges after just

---

* *God demonstrates His own love toward us, in that while we were yet sinners, Christ died for us.* (Romans 5:8, NASB)

seven days. We moved him cross-country twice in one week. We extended compassion, understanding, and love, but he paid the college class fees at college number two, because the Farrel Family Scholarship fund was out of money.

In all these cases, there was no malevolence, no rebellion, no bad attitudes, just youthful irresponsibility, so the answer to the need for the mulligan was love—and the new opportunity for our sons to be more responsible in round two. This kind of love assumes that when grace is given, grace will be lived out by the recipient.

There is a biblical mandate to give a mulligan, because we've all needed at least one: "[God] rescued us from the domain of darkness, and transferred us to the kingdom of His beloved Son, in whom we have redemption, the forgiveness of sins" (Colossians 1:13-14, NASB). Jesus transferred us over to a life in the light, but we are still imperfect people. He extends His grace and mercy to us daily, even when we might need a "mulligan" to get a restart or regroup in life.

If you've made a mistake or feel like you've botched up your life lately, ask Jesus for a mulligan and His wisdom to move you and your future back into the light where God designed you to live. I [Pam] begin each morning with a prayer, acknowledging my imperfection. I simply pray, "God, pour Your grace and mercy over me." Grace is God giving us the good things we don't deserve because of our imperfections. Mercy is God withholding the punishment we do deserve because of our sin. Pray God's grace, God's mercy, God's "mulligan" over your imperfections, and He will give you strength and more wisdom for life's journey.

❋ **Send Up a Message:** Lord, thank You for giving me a fresh start. I know my imperfection, and I praise You for giving me the opportunity to begin again and live for You. Amen.

❋ **Text Helps:** There's no better word than *rescue* for the person who is desperate in the dark. God rescues us to give us new life and direction! Be encouraged as you read these scriptures:
PSALM 107:20—[God] sent forth his word and healed them; he rescued them from the grave.

PSALM 116:1-8—I love the LORD, for he heard my voice; he heard my cry for mercy. Because he turned his ear to me, I will call on him as long as I live. The cords of death entangled me, the anguish of the grave came upon me; I was overcome by trouble and sorrow. Then I called on the name of the LORD: "O LORD, save me!" The LORD is gracious and righteous; our God is full of compassion. The LORD protects the simplehearted; when I was in great need, he saved me. Be at rest once more, O my soul, for the LORD has been good to you. For you, O LORD, have delivered my soul from death, my eyes from tears, my feet from stumbling.

2 TIMOTHY 4:18—The Lord will rescue me from every evil attack and will bring me safely to his heavenly kingdom. To him be glory for ever and ever. Amen.

❈ **Your Turn:** Write or text a message back to God about your life, what you read, or a request on your heart:

_____

_____

_____

_____

L O L

Country Club Call

Several men are in the locker room of a private club after finishing 18 holes. Suddenly a cell phone on one of the benches rings. A man picks it up, and the following conversation ensues:

"Hello? Honey, it's me."

"Sugar!"

"Are you at the club?"

"Yes."

"Great! I'm at the mall two blocks from where you are. I saw a beautiful mink coat. It's absolutely gorgeous! Can I buy it?"

"What's the price?"

"Only $1,500."

"Well, okay. Go ahead and get it, if you like it that much."

"Ahh . . . and I also stopped by the Mercedes dealership and saw this year's model at a really good price, and since we need to exchange the BMW that we bought last year . . ."

"What price did the salesman quote you?"

"Only $60,000."

"Okay, but for that price, I want it with all the options."

"Great! Before we hang up, there's something else . . ."

"What?"

"It might look like a lot, but I stopped by the real-estate office this morning and saw the house we looked at last year. It's on sale! Remember? The one with a pool, an English garden, a tennis court, an acre of park area, beach-front property . . ."

"How much are they asking?"

"Only $2 million; a fantastic price, and I see that we have that much in the bank to cover it."

"Well, then, go ahead and buy it, but just bid $1.8 million. Okay?"

"Okay, sweetie. Thanks! I'll see you later! I love you!"

"Bye!"

The man snaps the phone shut, raises his hand while holding the phone, and asks all those present, "Does anyone know who this phone belongs to?"[2]

1. Brent Kelley, "Golf History FAQ: Origin of 'Mulligan,'" About.com, http://golf.about.com/cs/historyofgolf/a/hist_mulligan.htm (accessed March 17, 2010).
2. Original source unknown. Adapted from "Cell Call," Jokes and Quotes, Golf'un, www.golfun.net/joke20.htm (accessed March 17, 2010).

Drawing a Blank

Text Message: *U wl cst al r sns nto t dpths of t c.* *

After speaking to a group of young women, I [Dawn] lingered to chat with a few of them. During one conversation, a 20-something mom asked me for my e-mail address and phone number. I leaned over and wrote down the e-mail address and then stood up and stared into space.

"Are you okay?" the woman asked with concern.

Embarrassed, I admitted, "I can't remember my phone number." I stood there nearly a minute—red-faced, drawing a blank, and making small talk while I commanded my gray matter to remember the digits! For sure, one frustrating challenge of getting older is forgetfulness.

But forgetting can also be a blessing. As a girl, I loved the story of brave Clara Barton, founder of the American Red Cross. But it wasn't until I became an adult that I realized how truly loving and kind she was. Once, when a friend reminded her of a slanderous accusation that someone had concocted against her years earlier, Clara replied, "I distinctly remember forgetting that."[1]

The reason Clara could forget was that she genuinely forgave. She refused to harbor a grudge and allow the poison of bitterness to build up in her heart. Instead, she purposely drew a blank.

I'm so grateful that God's forgiveness offers the blessing of new beginnings. When we're forgiven in Christ, we are righteous before God. Because of the Father's steadfast love and compassion, He pardons our sins. His forgiveness is complete. The Bible says He removes our sins as far as the east is from the west (Psalm 103:12). He buries them

---

* *You will cast all our sins into the depths of the sea.* (Micah 7:19, NKJV)

in the deepest sea. We can thank God that He chooses to draw a blank concerning our sin.

✸ **Send Up a Message:** Lord, thank You for Your abundant mercy! Show me how to forgive the way You forgive. Amen.

✸ **Text Helps:** Do you keep remembering a sin that the Lord has already forgiven? Faith is taking God at His Word. What He forgives is completely forgiven. Encourage your heart with these words:

PSALM 103:12—As far as the east is from the west, so far has he [God] removed our transgressions from us.

PSALM 130:3-4—If you, O LORD, kept a record of sins, O Lord, who could stand? But with you there is forgiveness; therefore you are feared.

JEREMIAH 31:33-34—"This is the covenant I will make with the house of Israel after that time," declares the LORD. "I will put my law in their minds and write it on their hearts. I will be their God, and they will be my people. . . . I will forgive their wickedness and will remember their sins no more."

MICAH 7:18-19—Who is a God like you, who pardons sin and forgives the transgression of the remnant of his inheritance? You do not stay angry forever but delight to show mercy. You will again have compassion on us; you will tread our sins underfoot and hurl all our iniquities into the depths of the sea.

✸ **Your Turn:** Write or text a message back to God about your life, what you read, or a request on your heart:

_____

_____

_____

_____

_____

_____

_____

L O L

State of Forgetfulness

An elderly couple had dinner at another couple's house, and after eating, the wives left the table and went into the kitchen. The two elderly gentlemen were talking, and one said, "Last night we went out to a new restaurant, and it was really great. I would recommend it very highly."

The other man said, "What is the name of the restaurant?"

The first man thought and thought and finally said, "What is the name of that flower you give to someone you love? You know . . . the one that is red and has thorns on it."

"Do you mean a rose?"

"Yes," the man said, and then he turned toward the kitchen and yelled, "Rose, what's the name of that restaurant we went to last night?"[2]

---

1. William E. Barton, *The Life of Clara Barton, Founder of the American Red Cross,* vol. 1 (Cambridge, MA: Houghton Mifflin, 1922), 345.
2. Original source unknown. Quoted in "A True Senior Moment," Humor of the Day, Bread Breakers, May 15, 2009, http://breadbreakers.typepad.com/bread_breakers_ministry/2009/05/humor-of-the-day-a-senior-moment .html (accessed March 17, 2010).

The Faith Connection

Text Message: *May th God o hp fil u w al jy & pec n blvng.* *

Imagine a hemorrhage that wouldn't stop for 12 years. This was the sad plight of a woman mentioned in the Bible (Mark 5:25-34). Weakened by the flow of blood, she spent her entire income but found no relief. She was desperate for help—perhaps about to lose all hope—when Jesus came to town. Mustering courage, she reached out to touch the Master's clothing as He passed by. She was healed in an instant.

She trembled in fear as Jesus turned around, and then she heard His tender words: "Daughter, your faith has made you well. Go in peace, and be healed of your affliction," (Mark 5:34, NKJV).

Though we may not fully understand why, sickness and physical devastation aren't always healed this side of heaven. Joni Eareckson Tada, a quadriplegic who turned her handicap into a ministry, once said, "I had to be healed of my desire to be healed."[1] Once her heart was yielded to God, she viewed suffering with a new perspective. "God is more concerned with conforming me to the likeness of His Son than leaving me in my comfort zones," she said. "The greatest good suffering can do for me is to increase my capacity for God."[2]

Because she allowed God to expand her capacity for seeing life from His point of view, Joni became a woman of joy and peace who shares biblical insight and wisdom with hurting people around the world through Joni and Friends.[3] What enabled such powerful ministry? It all began with her faith in God and His purposes for her life. God, the Author of hope, wants to fill you with His presence and power. It all begins with a faith connection.

---

* *May the God of hope fill you with all joy and peace in believing.* (Romans 15:13, ESV)

Maybe you can't control how the trauma or drama you are dealing with will work out, but you can control how you respond to it. Make a God connection and see how He might work in this seemingly impossible situation to bring you to a place of hope, joy, or peace.

✳ **Send Up a Message:** Teach me to trust You more, dear Father. Only You can satisfy my soul. Amen.

✳ **Text Helps:** The keyword in all of this is *connection*. We connect to God in faith and through prayer. As you read the following scriptures, ask the Lord to increase your faith today.

MARK 5:24-34—A large crowd followed and pressed around [Jesus]. And a woman was there who had been subject to bleeding for twelve years. She had suffered a great deal under the care of many doctors and had spent all she had, yet instead of getting better she grew worse. When she heard about Jesus, she came up behind him in the crowd and touched his cloak, because she thought, "If I just touch his clothes, I will be healed." Immediately her bleeding stopped and she felt in her body that she was freed from her suffering. At once Jesus realized that power had gone out from him. He turned around in the crowd and asked, "Who touched my clothes?" "You see the people crowding against you," his disciples answered, "and yet you can ask, 'Who touched me?'" But Jesus kept looking around to see who had done it. Then the woman, knowing what had happened to her, came and fell at his feet and, trembling with fear, told him the whole truth. He said to her, "Daughter, your faith has healed you. Go in peace and be freed from your suffering."

HEBREWS 10:38—My righteous one will live by faith. And if he shrinks back, I will not be pleased with him.

HEBREWS 11:6—Without faith it is impossible to please God, because anyone who comes to him must believe that he exists and that he rewards those who earnestly seek him.

❋ **Your Turn:** Write or text a message back to God about your life, what you read, or a request on your heart:

____

____

____

____

____

LOL

God Can Do It

Kari Voight shares a conversation her children had with their father:

> The other day my husband was driving our two-year-old, Bryan, and our five-year-old daughter, Brooke, home from daycare.
>
> Brooke said, "Daddy, today I prayed for two more sisters and another brother."
>
> My husband replied that it might be nice to have a larger family, but gently explained that it probably wouldn't happen.
>
> Brooke, who was seated behind him in the car, leaned forward and whispered in her daddy's ear, "How do you think I got Bryan?"[3]

❋ ❋ ❋

---

1. Joni Eareckson Tada, quoted in "Build Character," Suffering.net, www.suffering.net/buildch.htm (accessed March 17, 2010).
2. Joni Eareckson Tada, *When God Weeps: Why Our Sufferings Matter to the Almighty* (Grand Rapids: Zondervan, 1979), 121, 137.
3. To learn more about Joni and Friends, visit www.joniandfriends.org/.
4. Kari Voight, original article published in *Today's Christian Woman* (September–October 1997): 37, quoted in Pam Farrel, *Celebrate! I Made a Big Decision* (Colorado Springs: David C. Cook, 2000), 72.

Awaiting the Trip Home

Text Message: *4 r ctznshp s n hvn.* *

Long layovers in airports can be frustrating. The Farrels and Wilsons have had many such layovers, and we've learned to use our time wisely. In 2004, I [Dawn] couldn't imagine the pain of not being *able* to leave an airport until I saw a film.

In the comedy-drama *The Terminal,* actor Tom Hanks portrays Viktor Navorski, a traveler stranded at New York's JFK International Airport after a coup topples the government in his fictional homeland of Krakozhia. Carrying a defunct passport, Navorski is forced to hang around the airport until the conflict in his country is resolved. He learns to function in the airport, but he really doesn't fit in. The film is supposedly inspired by the true story of Mehran Nasseri's 18-year stay at Charles de Gaulle Airport in Paris.[1]

Christians are on one long layover, awaiting our trip home to heaven. We are aliens and strangers in this world. The ways and values of the world are foreign to us when we function as children of God. Sometimes we need to remind ourselves that we're not truly home yet. Our time here on earth is only temporary.

The big difference between Christian "aliens" and Navorski is that we're fighting battles on our own turf. The Evil One desires to destroy us, but Jesus prays for our protection (John 17:14-15) as we fight the battles that war against our souls (1 Peter 2:11) and wait for our heavenly home.

If you're feeling out of place here—if the sin, degradation, and brokenness of the world are weighing heavy on your heart—think of yourself

---

* *For our citizenship is in heaven, from which we also eagerly wait for the Savior, the Lord Jesus Christ.* (Philippians 3:20, NKJV)

as an ambassador, a representative of heaven serving in an alien land to help as many here as you can. When you think of yourself as an ambassador, time here on earth, though uncomfortable at times, gains a sense of purpose and nobility.

✳ **Send Up a Message:** I long for Your return, Lord. Help me get ready! Amen.

✳ **Text Helps:** We are just "passin' through" this world. If we are God's children, we're on our way to a better place. Look up Hebrews 11:9-16 and read about Abraham's desire for a heavenly city. Then read the following out-of-this-world truths.

JOHN 15:19—[Jesus said to His disciples,] "If you belonged to the world, it would love you as its own. As it is, you do not belong to the world, but I have chosen you out of the world. That is why the world hates you."

JOHN 17:14-15—[Jesus prayed,] "I have given them your word and the world has hated them, for they are not of the world any more than I am of the world. My prayer is not that you take them out of the world but that you protect them from the evil one."

1 PETER 2:11—Dear friends, I urge you, as aliens and strangers in the world, to abstain from sinful desires, which war against your soul.

✳ **Your Turn:** Write or text a message back to God about your life, what you read, or a request on your heart:

_____

_____

_____

_____

_____

_____

LOL

No Place Like Home

My [Dawn's] sister-in-law Robin shared this true story about her son Austin when he was a little boy:

> Oh, so very proud of his rich Texas heritage, my husband, Dennis, took the family to the Alamo in San Antonio to expose our children to this important part of our American history.
>
> After touring the grounds, we entered through the mission doors and felt an immediate churchlike reverence amid the rustic dirt-floor setting. Separated from the others, my four-year-old son and I peered into the various rooms.
>
> Standing in the doorway of a room that housed only a small wooden cannon trough and some old strewn hay, my little boy tugged at my hand and with a quiet little voice asked, "Mommy, is this where Jesus was born?"
>
> I paused, smiled, and responded, "No, my dear, but your father would like to think so."[2]

---

1. *The Terminal*, directed by Stephen Spielberg (Dreamworks Pictures, 2004).
2. Personal story shared by permission.

The Stars of Heaven

Text Message: *Yr lbr n t Lord s nt ftl.* *

Susan Boyle from Scotland became an overnight Internet celebrity. The plain-but-feisty 47-year-old contestant on the *Britain's Got Talent* television show transformed the audience at Clyde Auditorium in Glasgow, Scotland. At first, many mocked her frumpy appearance, but within seconds of Boyle's opening notes of "I Dreamed a Dream" from *Les Misérables*, the audience stood and gave her a wild ovation that continued for seven minutes. During the next nine days, more than 100 million people viewed various online videos of Boyle's amazing musical talent.[1]

Are there days when you feel insignificant? Perhaps as we gather before the throne of God, we'll be amazed at the so-called "nobodies" of this world who will stand out and shine like stars in heaven (1 Corinthians 1:26-31).

We'll hear stories of quiet prayer warriors who served by standing against Satan in prayer. We'll cheer for missionaries who served and sacrificed, often uncelebrated on earth; moms and dads who quietly modeled Christ and taught the Word to their children; Christian leaders who taught and lived the truth; a multitude of behind-the-scenes volunteers; all the persecuted and martyred believers of history—*every* good and faithful servant of God will be rewarded and hear God's "well done." It's all because of God's marvelous grace, and all praise will ultimately return to Him.

We want to encourage you to keep in mind that if you know Jesus, you're not a nobody.

---

* *Your labor in the* LORD *is not futile [it is never wasted or to no purpose].* (1 Corinthians 15:58, AMP)

"The righteous," the Bible says, "will shine like the sun in the kingdom of their Father" (Matthew 13:43). We will all reflect the splendor of our Lord, and enjoy Him forever. Remember, you are always a somebody to God.

❋ **Send Up a Message:** Father God, I want to please You and bring You glory, so I ask You to transform my life. Make me more like Your Son. Amen.

❋ **Text Helps:** Read 1 Corinthians 1:26-31 to get a perspective on who God says are the standouts in heaven. Then, as you read the following verses, ask God to give you a greater understanding of what will make you a shining star for Him.

DANIEL 12:3—Those who are wise will shine like the brightness of the heavens, and those who lead many to righteousness, like the stars for ever and ever.

MATTHEW 6:20—Store up for yourselves treasures in heaven, where moth and rust do not destroy, and where thieves do not break in and steal.

1 CORINTHIANS 9:24-25—Do you not know that in a race all the runners run, but only one gets the prize? Run in such a way as to get the prize. Everyone who competes in the games goes into strict training. They do it to get a crown that will not last; but we do it to get a crown that will last forever.

❋ **Your Turn:** Write or text a message back to God about your life, what you read, or a request on your heart:

____

____

____

____

____

____

____

LOL

Memorable Moment

Our friend Holly has a darling five-year-old girl who is always saying memorable things, which sometimes sound far above her age level.

While at an amusement park with family friends, including a teenage son who had caught the eye of Holly's daughter, the little girl reached over and gave the mother of the son a necklace she had found at the park. As she handed the necklace to the mom she said, "Please give this to your son. It's something to remember me by."[2]

1. "Susan Boyle Breaks Past 100 Million Online Views," Fan Fare, Reuters.com, April 20, 2009, http://blogs.reuters.com/fanfare/2009/04/20/susan-boyle-breaks-past-100-million-online-views/(accessed March 17, 2010).
2. Holly Hanson, personal story shared with authors. Used by permission.

The Last Laugh

Text Message: *"B of gd chr; I hv ovrcm th wrld."**

I [Dawn] remember the day I saw artist Jack Jewell's rendition of *The Risen Christ by the Sea*.[1] The Jesus in the painting stood on an old ship by the Sea of Tiberias as in John 21:1. His mouth was open in a hearty, manly laugh.

"Yes!" I said. "The Bible tells me that Jesus wept (John 11:35) and that He had righteous anger (Matthew 21:12-13; Mark 3:5). Surely He must have laughed, too." Jesus had human emotions, but they were always based in His holy character.

"Despised and rejected by men, a Man of sorrows and acquainted with grief" (Isaiah 53:3-4, NKJV), Jesus was a serious man on a mission, who prayed, taught, healed, and suffered. But He was also the tender Jesus who welcomed little children, and I imagine Him laughing at their childish play (Mark 10:13-14). Perhaps He smiled at Peter's sanguine outbursts or joked with His disciples as He taught them life-changing stories.

Jesus, who overcame the world (John 16:33), would also believe that "a happy heart is good medicine" (Proverbs 17:22, AMP). He must have believed in joy because He taught it, referencing it often in His famous Sermon on the Mount as He declared truths like: "The kingdom of heaven is like treasure hidden in a field. When a man found it, he hid it again, and then in his joy went and sold all he had and bought that field" (Matthew 13:44).

As Jesus hung on the cross, Satan may have laughed, ignoring the implications of the Savior's words, "It is finished" (John 19:30); but *Jesus had the last laugh*. His words were a mighty declaration of victory.

---

* [Jesus said,] *"Be of good cheer, I have overcome the world."* (John 16:33, NKJV)

We need to be serious about our faith, but we also want to live joy-filled lives. Remember, God created our funny bones! Jesus, though fully God, was also fully human. He was an extraordinary human, and we think He must have had wonderful moments of laughter as He walked this earth.

❋ **Send Up a Message:** Father God, I thank You for the gift of humor and for the many ways You've given me to express my love for You and others. I'm so glad Jesus freed us from sin's power! Amen.

❋ **Text Helps:** We can rejoice because Jesus triumphed on the cross and then rose from the dead to declare victory over Satan, death, and sin! Rejoice in our wonderful Savior as you read the following scriptures:
PROVERBS 17:22—A happy heart is good medicine and a cheerful mind works healing. (AMP)
JOHN 15:11; 16:33—[Jesus said,] "I have told you this so that my joy may be in you and that your joy may be complete. . . . I have told you these things, so that in me you may have peace. In this world you will have trouble. But take heart! I have overcome the world."
COLOSSIANS 2:13-15—When you were dead in your sins . . . God made you alive with Christ. He forgave us all our sins, having canceled the written code, with its regulations, that was against us and that stood opposed to us; he took it away, nailing it to the cross. And having disarmed the powers and authorities, he made a public spectacle of them, triumphing over them by the cross.
1 PETER 1:3-4, 8—Praise be to the God and Father of our Lord Jesus Christ! In his great mercy he has given us new birth into a living hope through the resurrection of Jesus Christ from the dead, and into an inheritance that can never perish, spoil or fade—kept in heaven for you. . . . Even though you do not see him [Jesus] now, you believe in him and are filled with an inexpress-ible and glorious joy.

✻ **Your Turn:** Write or text a message back to God about your life, what you read, or a request on your heart:

_____

_____

_____

_____

LOL

Eager Encouragement

Charlotte Adelsperger, coauthor of *Through the Generations: The Unique Call of Motherhood,* found herself in an embarrassing situation when all she wanted to do was encourage someone:

> At church, I am always looking for ways to connect with others and encourage them. As I entered a Sunday school classroom, ahead of me was a young woman carrying an attractive gift bag with bright tissue.
>
> "That's a cute package you're carrying," I commented.
>
> When she turned around, I noticed she wore a very full maternity dress. "You mean this?" she said, patting her abdomen.[2]

1. To purchase a copy of Jack Jewell's print, visit *The Joyful Noiseletter* at www.joyfulnoiseletter.com/risen_Christ.asp.
2. Charlotte Adelsperger, personal correspondence with authors. Used by permission.

About the Authors

Pam Farrel is known for "choosin' joy!" Her messages of hope and help have encouraged and equipped women worldwide. Pam and her husband, Bill, are international speakers, relationship experts on marriage and parenting, and are the authors of over 30 books, including best-selling *Men Are Like Waffles, Women Are Like Spaghetti.* Pam has written numerous books for women, including *The 10 Best Decisions a Woman Can Make, Woman of Influence, Woman of Confidence,* and *Fantastic After 40.* Pam is also the founder and president of Seasoned Sisters, an organization designed to encourage and equip women to maximize mid-life and beyond. For more information, go to www.seasonedsisters.com. Bill and Pam Farrel have relationship columns in magazines and newspapers, are frequent guests on radio and TV, and their resources have been translated into more than 15 languages. The Farrels have experience as a pastoral couple and are available for speaking engagements. Pam is also a popular speaker for women's events. She and Bill have parented three children and enjoy their relationship with their daughter-in-law and granddaughters. When Pam is not writing, she is looking for her car keys, cell phone, or ginko. She wants her audiences to know "U R cr8ed 2 b gr8 4 God."

To contact the Farrels:
Farrel Communications
3755 Avocado Blvd. #414
La Mesa, CA 91941
(800) 810-4449
http://www.farrelcommunications.com

Dawn Wilson's passion in life is wrapped up in one word: *Choices!* Whether encouraging women to make daily choices that align with God's Word, or pointing them to the one crucial decision in life— "What will you do with Jesus?"—Dawn offers wisdom that makes women think and hope in Christ that heals their hearts. Though this is her first book, Dawn's writing career began in the 1980s as a freelance writer for *Spirit of Revival* magazine. She also worked as a journalist for 16 years with San Diego's *Christian Examiner*. She currently serves as a writer and researcher for *Revive Our Hearts* radio teacher Nancy Leigh DeMoss; writes for a prophecy-focused television ministry; and serves as Communications Director for Pam Farrel's Seasoned Sisters. Dawn and her husband founded the leadership-development organization PaceSetter Ministries, and Dawn later founded her own speaking outreach, Heart Choices Ministries. The Wilsons, married 36 years, are glad their two grown sons and their families live in San Diego so they can enjoy their three granddaughters. "Life is all about choices," Dawn says. "I choose God, family, bookstore gift cards, and rich dark chocolate!"

MINISTRIES

Statement of Purpose:

Heart Choices Ministries was founded to encourage women to make proactive choices that build a life of excellence to the glory of God. This is accomplished as women discover the heart of God in the Word of God, and then pursue godliness, wisdom, and truth in every area of life.

Practical Application:

Dawn encourages women to do three things:

- *Be Transparent*—"Recognize past choices. They have made you who you are."
- *Be Truthful*—"Examine where you are today. Are you willing to change?"
- *Be Transformed*—"Embrace hope! Pursue a life of excellence with new choices."

"Our choices reveal our hearts, and we can always change those choices to align closer to the heart of God."—Dawn

Endorsements:

"Dawn is expressive in her love for God and His Word. Through her teaching, speaking, and writing, her warmth and personal interest in women connect their hearts to hers immediately. You will go away challenged in your faith for a deeper walk with Jesus."

 —Darlene Barber, Women's Ministries, Shadow Mountain
  Community Church

"Dawn has her finger on the pulse of what is happening in the hearts of women because she serves in the trenches on the frontlines of ministry today. She is positive, biblical, challenging, and encouraging. Every woman will benefit from the sound, authentic, compelling, and caring message God has placed on Dawn's heart."

 —Pam Farrel, speaker and author of *Men Are Like Waffles,*
  Women Are Like Spaghetti

Contact Information:

Dawn Wilson
Heart Choices Ministries
P.O. Box 21669, El Cajon, CA 92021
dawn@heartchoicesministries.com

Blog: http://heartchoicestoday.blogspot.com
Facebook: www.facebook.com/DawnMarieWilson
Twitter: http://twitter.com/heartchoices
Free monthly newsletter: "Choices, Choices, Choices"

FOCUS ON THE FAMILY®

Welcome to the Family

Whether you purchased this book, borrowed it or received it as a gift, we're glad you're reading it. It's just one of the many helpful, encouraging and biblically based resources produced by Focus on the Family® for people in all stages of life.

Focus began in 1977 with the vision of one man, Dr. James Dobson, a licensed psychologist and author of numerous best-selling books on marriage, parenting and family. Alarmed by the societal, political and economic pressures that were threatening the existence of the American family, Dr. Dobson founded Focus on the Family with one employee and a once-a-week radio broadcast aired on 36 stations.

Now an international organization reaching millions of people daily, Focus on the Family is dedicated to preserving values and strengthening and encouraging families through the life-changing message of Jesus Christ.

Focus on the Family
MAGAZINES

These faith-building, character-developing publications address the interests, issues, concerns, and challenges faced by every member of your family from preschool through the senior years.

For More
INFORMATION

 ONLINE:
Log on to
FocusOnTheFamily.com
In Canada, log on to
FocusOnTheFamily.ca

 PHONE:
Call toll-free:
**800-A-FAMILY
(232-6459)**
In Canada, call toll-free:
800-661-9800

| **THRIVING FAMILY™**
Marriage & Parenting | **FOCUS ON THE FAMILY CLUBHOUSE JR.®**
Ages 4 to 8 | **FOCUS ON THE FAMILY CLUBHOUSE®**
Ages 8 to 12 | **FOCUS ON THE FAMILY CITIZEN®**
U.S. news issues | Rev. 4/10 |

More Great Resources
from Focus on the Family®

Raising a Modern-Day Princess: Inspiring Purpose, Value, and Strength in Your Daughter
By Pam Farrel & Doreen Hanna
In an easy-to-use, step-by-step style, Pam Farrel and Doreen Hanna show moms how to create a life-changing rite of passage experience for their daughters, celebrating their crossover into womanhood. With personal stories and advice from real moms, this book will help you raise *your* modern-day princess.

When Moms Pray Together: True Stories of God's Power to Transform Your Child
By Fern Nichols
These gritty, moving stories from around the world reveal God's power in the midst of life's greatest trials and give you strategies for biblical, effective prayers. *When Moms Pray Together* provides hope, the will to persevere in prayer, and encouragement to praying moms everywhere.

No More Headaches: Enjoying Sex & Intimacy in Marriage
By Dr. Juli Slattery
Dr. Juli Slattery offers honest answers to the questions wives are afraid to ask. With warmth and compassion, she helps women understand the sexual differences between men and women and offers practical advice for those who want to strengthen—or save—their marriages.

FOR MORE INFORMATION

 Online:
Log on to FocusOnTheFamily.com
In Canada, log on to FocusOnTheFamily.ca

 Phone:
Call toll-free: 800-A-FAMILY
In Canada, call toll-free: 800-661-9800

BPZZXP1